THE SUPREME COURT AND THE FEDERAL JUDICIARY

The Supreme Court and the Federal Judiciary

Steven C. Caldwell (Editor)

Nova Science Publishers, Inc.
New York

Senior Editors: Susan Boriotti and Donna Dennis
Coordinating Editor: Tatiana Shohov
Office Manager: Annette Hellinger
Graphics: Wanda Serrano
Editorial Production: Jennifer Vogt, Matthew Kozlowski, Jonathan Rose and Maya Columbus
Circulation: Ave Maria Gonzalez, Vera Popovich, Luis Aviles, Raymond Davis, Melissa Diaz, Vladimir Klestov and Jeannie Pappas
Marketing: Cathy DeGregory

Library of Congress Cataloging-in-Publication Data
Available Upon Request

ISBN: 1-59033-388-8.

400 Oser Ave, Suite 1600
Hauppauge, New York 11788-3619
Tele. 631-231-7269 Fax 631-231-8175
e-mail: Novascience@earthlink.net
Web Site: http://www.novapublishers.com

Printed in the United States of America

CONTENTS

PREFACE

Hogue, in his chapter, examines the 152 nominations to the U.S. Supreme Court between 1789 and 2001, of which 32 were not confirmed by the Senate. The 32 nominations represent 27 individuals who failed to be confirmed the first time they were nominated, however, three were later nominated again and confirmed. The Supreme Court nominations discussed here were not confirmed for a variety of reasons, including Senate opposition to the nominating President, nominee's views, or incumbent Court; senatorial courtesy; perceived political unreliability of the nominee; perceived lack of ability; interest group opposition; and fear of altering the balance of the Court. The Senate Committee on the Judiciary has played an important role in the confirmation process, particularly since 1868.

There have been calls for change in the Supreme Court directed at three aspects of the Supreme Court appointment process: the involvement of outside interest groups; the overall length of time taken by the process; and the process by which the Senate as a whole decides whether to confirm or reject the President's nominee. Rutkus analyzes these topics along with recess appointments of federal judges and profession qualifications for appointment to the federal judiciary.

Following this discussion, Morgan addresses the question of whether there is a requirement that federal judges be lawyers. The answer is that there are no constitutional provisions setting forth professional qualifications for appointees to the judiciary. The very few statutory professional prerequisites apply only to nominees to federal courts whose judges are not constitutionally entitled to "good Behaviour" tenure.

Fisher concludes with a chapter discussing the history and contentious issues surrounding the recess appointments of judges. Included in the study is the meaning of the Recess Clause, Senate prerogatives, and the opportunity of a litigant in federal court to have a case handled by a judge with full independence.

Chapter 1

SUPREME COURT NOMINATIONS NOT CONFIRMED, 1789-2001

Henry B. Hogue

Over the course of United States history, approximately one-quarter of the presidential nominations to the U.S. Supreme Court have failed to place a new Associate or Chief Justice on the bench. Of the 152 nominations to the Court between 1789 and 2001, 112 individuals were confirmed and served, seven individuals were confirmed and declined to serve, one confirmed nominee died before he could take his seat, and 32 nominations were not confirmed. This chapter discusses this last group of Supreme Court nominations. These 32 nominations represent 27 individuals whose names were sent forward to the Senate by Presidents (some of those 27 individuals were nominated more than once). The Supreme Court nominations discussed here were not confirmed for a variety of reasons, including Senate opposition to the nominating President, the nominee's views, or the incumbent Court; senatorial courtesy; perceived political unreliability of the nominee; perceived lack of ability; interest group opposition; and fear of altering the balance of the Court. The Senate Committee on the Judiciary has played an important role in the confirmation process, particularly since 1868.

Summary discussions of the Senate confirmation process and the unsuccessful nominations follow. The reasons some nominations have failed confirmation and the role of the Senate Judiciary Committee are also discussed. Finally, the chapter includes a detailed table that identifies each nomination and provides, for each, the facts that can be documented about the dates of relevant activity and votes in the Judiciary Committee and the full Senate. A list of additional literature regarding unsuccessful nominations is also provided.

THE CONFIRMATION PROCESS

The Constitution of the United States provides for the appointment of a Justice to the Supreme Court an Article II, Section 2. This section states that the President "shall nominate, and by and with the Advice and Consent of the Senate, shall appoint... Judges of the [S]upreme Court." The practices involved in following this consitutional mandate have varied over the years, but they have always involved the sharing of the appointment power between the President and the Senate.[1]

Nominations that failed to be confirmed by the Senate have been disposed of in a variety of ways, including withdrawal by the President, inaction in the committee, inaction in the Senate, postponement, tabling, rejection on the Senate floor, and filibuster on the Senate floor. **Table 1** provides a summary of the unsuccessful nominations by final disposition.

Table 1. Supreme Court Nominations not Confirmed, 1789-2000, by Final Disposition

Rejected by a vote of the full Senate	11
Withdrawn by the President without Senate action	2
Postponed or tabled by the Senate, but no withdrawn by the President	5
Postponed or tabled by the Senate and withdrawn by the President	3
No record of referral or other action	2
Referred to committee, but never reported or discharged from committee	4
Reported or discharged from committee, not acted on by the full Senate	2
Reported or discharged from committee, withdrawn by the President	2
Filibustered, withdrawn by the President	1
Total Supreme Court nominations not confirmed	32

[1] For a more detailed history of the Supreme Court nominations process, see CRS Report 94-355 GOV, *Supreme Court Appointment Process*, by Denis Steven Rutkus; and CRS Report 94-479 GOV, *Senate Judiciary Committee Consideration of Supreme Court Nominations*, by Denis Steven Rutkus.

SUMMARY OF UNSUCCESSFUL NOMINATIONS

The 32 Supreme Court nominations not confirmed by the Senate represent 27 individuals. Three of these 27 were later re-nominated and confirmed for positions on the Court. Of the other 24 nominees, four were nominated and failed confirmation more than once. **Table 2** provides summary information concerning unsuccessful nominations.

The first of the three nominees who were not confirmed only to be later renominated and confirmed was William Paterson, nominated by President George Washington. Washington withdrew the nomination on the day following its submission. He noted that Paterson "was a member of the Senate when the law creating that office was passed, and that the time for which he was elected [had] not yet expired."[2] For this reason, President Washington felt that the nomination was in violation of the Constitution.[3] President Washington re-nominated Paterson at the beginning of the following Congress a few days later, and Paterson was immediately confirmed.[4] All of the other unsuccessful nominations faced opposition in the Senate.

---

[2] U.S. Congress, Senate, *Journal of the Executive Proceedings of the Senate of the United States of America,* vol. 1, p. 135. (Hereafter cited as *Executive Journal.)*

[3] Article I, Section 6 of the Constitution provides that, "No Senator or Representative shall, during the Time for which he was elected, be appointment to any civil Office... , which shall have been created... during such time..." the office to which Washington was nominating Paterson, Associate Justice, was created by the Judiciary Act of 1789 on September 24, 1789, during which time Paterson was a Senator. Paterson began serving in the Senate on March 4, 1789 and resigned on November 13, 1790, having been elected Governor of New Jersey (U.S. Congress, House, *Biographical Directory of the American Congress,* H. Doc. 607, 81st Cong., 2nd sess. [Washington: GPO, 1950], p. 1655). His term, however, did not conclude until March 3, 1793 (U.S. Congress, Senate, *Senate Manual,* S.Doc. 106-1, 106th Cong., 1st sess. [Washington: GPO, 2000], p. 859), and so his appointment to Associate Justice prior to that date would have been unconstitutional. President Washington re-nominated, and a special session of the Senate of the new Congress confirmed, Paterson on March 4, 1793. Paterson's Senate position had covered four years, rather than six, due to the staggering of Senate terms at the outset of the First Congress, which was called for in the Constitution (Article I, Section 3) and was implemented in the Senate in May 1789.

[4] *Executive Journal,* vol. 1, p. 139.

Table 2. Summary of Supreme Court Nominations Not Confirmed, 1789-2001[5]

Total Supreme Court nominations	152
Total Supreme Court nominations not confirmed	32
Nominees who failed to be confirmed at least once	27
Unconfirmed nominees who never served in the position to which they were nominated	24
Unconfirmed nominees later re-nominated and confirmed	3
Nominees subject to two or three failed nominations (for a total of nine nominations)	4
Unconfirmed nomination to elevate sitting Associate Justice to Chief Justice	1
Unconfirmed nomination of former Associate Justice to Chief Justice	1

The other two nominees who were later re-nominated and confirmed were Roger B. Taney, nominated twice by President Andrew Jackson, and Stanley Matthews, nominated first by President Rutherford B. Hayes and later by President James A. Garfield. Taney's first nomination, to Associate Justice, was postponed indefinitely by the Senate. During the next Congress, he was nominated and confirmed as Chief Justice, and he went on to author the *Dred Scott* decision. Matthews' first nomination was never reported out of committee, but in the following Congress, under a new President, he was re-nominated and confirmed by a one-vote margin.[6]

Four individuals were the subjects of more than one unsuccessful nomination. The first three, John C. Spencer, Reuben H. Walworth, and Edward King, were nominees of President John Tyler. President Tyler had the opportunity to fill two vacancies on the high court. He made nine nominations of five men in the space of the last 15 months of his presidency. Eight of these nominations were not confirmed, giving President Tyler the highest tally of unconfirmed Supreme Court nominations. President Tyler nominated Spencer for the first vacancy. After the Senate rejected Spencer, Walworth was put forward for the position, and the Senate tabled this nomination. On June 17, 1844, the last day of the congressional session,[7] President Tyler withdrew the tabled Walworth nomination and re-

[5] Total Supreme Court nominations calculated using data from Elder Witt, *Guide to the U.S. Supreme Court*, 2nd ed. (Washington: Congressional Quarterly, 1990), pp. 995-998; and Lee Epstein, Jeffrey A. Segal, Harold J. Spaeth, and Thomas G. Walker, *The Supreme Court Compendium: Data, Decisions, and Developments* (Washington: Congressional Quarterly, 1994), pp. 284-290. Other totals summarize information from Table 4 of this report.

[6] *Executive Journal*, vol. 23, pp. 14, 75-76.

[7] 28th Congress, 1st Sess.

nominated Spencer. Unable to gain unanimous consent for the Spencer nomination to be acted upon, Tyler then withdrew Spencer's name on the same day and re-nominated Walworth.[8] By this time, the nomination (June 5, 1844) of King for the second vacancy had also been tabled. Tyler went on to re-nominate Walworth and King at the beginning of the following congressional session. After these two nominations were once again tabled, they were both withdrawn. The nomination of John M. Read, which followed, was reported out of committee but never acted upon by the full Senate. Samuel Nelson was President Tyler's fifth nominee, and he was confirmed.

The fourth individual subject to multiple unconfirmed nominations was William B. Hornblower, who was nominated in successive sessions of Congress by President Grover Cleveland. His first nomination was never reported out of committee; the second nomination was reported out and rejected.

One of the unsuccessful nominees had previously been Associate Justice, had left the Court, and this time was being nominated for Chief Justice. Another was a sitting Associate Justice nominated for elevation to the Chief Justice position. The first of these was also the first nomination in which the Senate voted not to confirm. John Rutledge had previously served as one of the first Associate Justices from 1789 to 1791. In addition, he served as Chief Justice in 1795 under a recess appointment by President Washington. When the President nominated him later that year to succeed John Jay as permanent Chief Justice, however, the Senate asserted its constitutional power and voted against confirmation. The second such nominee, Justice Abe Fortas, was a sitting Associate Justice at the time of his nomination by President Lyndon B. Johnson to be Chief Justice in 1968. The nomination was favorably reported out of committee but filibustered on the floor of the Senate until the President withdrew the nomination.

One unsuccessful nomination coincided with a legislative initiative to decrease the size of the Court. On April 16, 1866, President Andrew Johnson nominated Henry Stanbery to replace John Carton, who had died the previous May. By the time Stanbery was nominated, however, the House of Representatives had passed a bill decreasing the number of justices in the Supreme Court.[9] The act, as signed into law on July 23, 1866, called for a decrease in the number of Associate Justices from nine to six through the process of attrition.[10] At the time the bill was initiated and also at the time its final version

---

[8] "Washington: Adjournment of Congress," *Daily National Intelligencer* (Washington), June 18, 1844, p. 3.

[9] H.R. 334 (39th Congress), passed Mar. 8, 1866.

[10] An Act to fix the Number of Judges of the Supreme Court of the United States, and to change certain Judicial Circuits, *Statutes at large* 14, chap. 210, sec. 1, p. 209 (1866).

was signed, only one vacancy, that to which Stanbery was nominated, existed on the Court. Eight Associate Justice positions remained on the bench until the death of James M. Wayne in July 1867. Seven Associate Justice positions remained until a law was passed in April 1869 to increase the number back to eight.[11]

Several scholars have suggested that, by reducing the number of Associate Justice positions,[12] the Republican Congress was trying to thwart the ability of Democratic President Johnson to shape the Supreme Court, although the record of House and Senate debate is silent as to each chamber's intention in this regard.[13] The law increasing the Associate Justice positions to eight was passed within two months of the beginning of the Administration of President Ulysses S. Grant.

FACTORS BEHIND UNSUCCESSFUL NOMINATIONS

There have often been multiple reasons behind the failure of the Senate to confirm a nomination. The official Senate records, particularly those prior to the twentieth century, have usually been silent on the issues involved. Scholars have used other records in an effort to shed more light on the factors underlying unsuccessful Supreme Court nominations. This scholarship consists of analysis and interpretation of these records, and it provides a general understanding of the reasons that more than one in five nominations has failed to be confirmed by the Senate.

One widely cited scholar in the area of the Supreme Court appointments process and history, Henry J Abraham, has developed categories of unsuccessful nominations:

> Among the more prominent reasons have been: (1) opposition to the nominating president, not necessarily the nominee; (2) the nominee's involvement with one or more contentious issues of public policy or, simply, opposition to the nominee's perceived jurisprudential or sociopolitical philosophy (i.e., politics); (3) opposition to the record of the incumbent

---

[11] An Act to amend the Judicial System of the United States, *Statutes at Large* 15, chap. 22, sec. 1, p. 44 (1869).

[12] See Joseph P. Harris, *The Advice and Consent of the Senate* (New York: Greenwood Press, 1968), p. 304; Henry J. Abraham, *Justices and Presidents,* 3rd ed. (New York: Oxford University Press, 1992), pp. 124-125; and J. Myron Jacobstein and Roy M. Mersky, *The Rejected: Sketches of the 26 Men Nominated for the Supreme Court but Not Confirmed by the Senate* (Milpitas, CA: Toucan Valley Publications, 1993), pp. 67-74.

[13] See "Supreme Court of the United states," *The Congressional Globe,* vol. 72, Mar. 8, 1866, p. 1259; "Supreme Court Judges," *The Congressional Globe,* vol. 74, July 10, 1866, p. 3697; "United States Supreme Court," *The Congressional Globe,* vol. 75, July 18, 1866, p. 3909.

Court, which, rightly or wrongly, the nominee presumably supported; (4) senatorial courtesy (closely linked to the consultative nominating process); (5) a nominee's perceived political unreliability on the part of the party in power; (6) the evident lack of qualification or limited ability of the nominee; (7) concerted, sustained opposition by interest or pressure groups; and (8) fear that the nominee would dramatically alter the Court's jurisprudential lineup.[14]

The sections below discuss the nominations with respect to these categories based on the preponderance of scholarly evidence. Many of the nominations fall into multiple categories.

Opposition to the President

Opposition to the nominating President played a role in at least 16 of the 32 nominations that were not confirmed. Many of the 16 were put forward by Presidents in the last year of their presidency — seven occurred after a successor President had been elected, but before the transfer of power to the new administration. Each of these "lame duck" nominations transpired under nineteenth-century Presidents when the post-election period lasted from early November until early March. Four one-term Presidents made these nominations. President John Quincy Adams nominated John J. Crittenden in December 1828, after losing the election to Andrew Jackson.[15] President Tyler's third nomination of Walworth, second nomination of King, and only nomination of Read all came after Tyler had lost to James Polk.[16] President Millard Fillmore nominated George E. Badger and William C. Micou after Franklin Pierce had been elected to replace him.[17] Finally, President James Buchanan forwarded the name of Jeremiah S. Black to the Senate less than a month before Abraham Lincoln's inauguration.[18] Other nominations where opposition to the President was a major factor include the remaining unsuccessful Tyler nominations, Fillmore's

---

[14] Abraham, p. 39.

[15] Charles Warren, *The Supreme Court in United States History,* revised edition, vol. 1 (Boston: Little, Brown, and Company, 1926), pp. 701-704; William F. Swindler, "The Politics of 'Advice and Consent,'" *American Bar Association Journal*, v. 56, 1970, p. 537.

[16] Warren, vol. 2, pp. 115-120; Swindler, pp. 537-538. Notably, Tyler also put forth his one successful nomination out of nine, of Samuel Nelson, a month before the transfer of power.

[17] Warren, vol. 2, pp. 242-245; Swindler, pp. 538-539.

[18] Warren, vol. 2, pp. 363-365.

nomination of Edward A. Bradford, and Andrew Johnson's nomination of Henry Stanbery.[19]

President Lyndon B. Johnson's two unsuccessful nominations (Fortas and Thornberry) occurred during the last seven months of his presidency, when, having announced he was not seeking re-election, he was considered by some to be a lame duck even before the election of his successor. Nineteen Senators issued a statement indicating that, on this basis, they would oppose any nomination by President Johnson.[20] The committee report accompanying the nomination of Abe Fortas to Chief Justice, however, suggests that the opposition to Justice Fortas was based, to a considerable extent, on concern about money received by Fortas for delivering university lectures while an Associate Justice, Fortas's close relationship and advisory role with President Johnson while an Associate Justice, and his judicial philosophy.[21]

President Rutherford B. Hayes nominated Stanley Matthews in late January 1881, about six weeks before the transfer of power to the Garfield administration. In this case, however, the opposition seems to have centered on the nominee and his views, as discussed below, rather than on the nominating President.

Opposition to the Nominee's Views

President Washington's nomination of John Rutledge to Chief Justice, in 1975, was the first unsuccessful nomination to fail based on the nominee's political views. Shortly after his nomination, Rutledge made a strong speech denouncing the controversial and newly ratified Jay treaty between the United States and Great Britain. The Senate, which was dominated by Federalists and had ratified the treaty, rejected the Rutledge nomination. Of the 14 who voted for rejection, 13 were Federalists, putting them in the position of rejecting a nomination by a President from their own party.[22]

Alexander Wolcott's nomination 15 years later was the next to be rejected by the Senate. Wolcott's strong enforcement of the controversial embargo and non-

[19] Abraham, pp. 39-41, 124-125. As previously discussed, Congress initiated legislation to reduce the number of Associate Justices around the time of Stanbery's nomination.

[20] Jacobstein and Mersky, pp. 131-132.

[21] U.S. Congress, Senate Committee on the Judiciary, *Nomination of Abe Fortas,* report to accompany the nomination of Abe Fortas, 90th Cong., 2nd sess. Exec. Rept. 8. (Washington: GPO, 1968).

[22] See Warren, vol. 1, pp. 129-139; Harris, pp. 42-43; Ruth Bader Ginsburg, "Confirming Supreme Court Justices: Thoughts on the Second Opinion Rendered by the Senate," *University of Illinois Law review,* Winter 1988, p. 101-117, at 106; Swindler, pp. 534-535.

intercourse acts while a U.S. collection of customs cost him support in the press and the Senate. His qualifications for the position were also questioned.[23]

Andrew Jackson's first nomination of Roger B. Taney in 1835 was the third nomination for which the lack of success is often attributed to the nominee's views. In this case, there was also opposition to the nominating President's politics. Prior to the nomination, President Jackson had given a recess appointment to Taney to be Secretary of the Treasure. In that capacity, Taney had, under Jackson's direction, removed the government's deposits from the United States Bank. Jackson's Whig opponents in the Senate were incensed by this move, and this led first to the rejection of Taney as permanent Secretary of the Treasure and then to the failure of his first nomination to the Court. [24]

President James Polk's nomination of George W. Woodward in 1845 was rejected when six Democrats, led by a Senator from the nominee's home state of Pennsylvania, joined with the Whigs to oppose it. Woodward's nativist views are cited for the failure of his nomination.[25]

Ebenezer R. Hoar served as President Ulysses S. Grant's Attorney General prior to his nomination to be Associate Justice in 1869. In that capacity, Hoar had alienated Senators by recommending to Grant nominees for Circuit Judge without regard for the Senators' preference. In addition, the majority of the Senate disliked "his active labors on behalf of a merit civil service system for the federal government... and his opposition to Andrew Johnson's impeachment."[26] Despite praise for Hoar's nomination in the press, the Senate rejected it.

Stanley Matthews was nominated first by President Rutherford B. Hayes in 1881, in the last weeks of Hayes' presidency. The Senate opposed the nomination because of Matthews' close ties to railroad and financial interests, and the Judiciary Committee postponed the nomination. Although Matthews was subsequently re-nominated by President James Garfield and confirmed, concerns about him persisted, and the Senate vote, at 24-23, was the closest for any successful nominee.[27]

The first unsuccessful nominee in the twentieth century was rejected by the Senate in large part because of opposition to his perceived views. John J. Parker, nominated by President Herbert Hoover in 1930, was opposed by the National Association for the Advancement of Colored People (NAACP) and organized

---

[23] Warren, vol. 1, pp. 410-413; Swindler, pp. 535-536; Abraham, pp. 41, 88.
[24] Harris, pp. 59-64; Warren, vol. 1, pp. 798-802.
[25] Abraham, pp. 41, 109; Warren, vol. 2, pp. 146-147; Harris, p. 69.
[26] Abraham, p. 127. See also Warren, vol. 2, pp. 501-504, 507; Harris, pp. 74-75.
[27] Warren, vol. 2, pp. 622-623; Abraham 135-137.

labor based on his previous statements and writings.[28] The NAACP testified in opposition to Parker's racial views at his confirmation hearing. Their testimony was based on a statement Parker had made in the course of an unsuccessful campaign for governor of North Carolina in 1920, in which he opposed the participation of African-Americans in politics.[29] In addition, Parker's record on labor issues, as chief judge of the U.S. Fourth Circuit Court of Appeals, was criticized by labor at the hearing. The American Federation of Labor (AFL), representing several labor groups, objected in particular to an opinion, authored by Parker, that affirmed a lower court opinion in support of "yellow dog" contracts, in which employees agreed not to join a union as a condition of employment.[30]

As noted previously, President Lyndon B. Johnson's nomination of Justice Abe Fortas in 1968 for elevation to Chief Justice failed for several reasons, including his judicial philosophy. Although the Committee on the Judiciary reported the nomination favorably, several committee members strongly dissented in the committee's printed report. One Senator wrote that Fortas's "judicial philosophy disqualifies him for this high office." Another criticized Fortas as part of the majority on the Supreme Court led by Chief Justice Earl Warren (the Warren Court) making an "extremist effort to set itself up as a super-legislature." A Third Senator also found Fortas lacking on the "broader question of the nominee's judicial philosophy which includes his willingness to subject himself to the restraint inherent in the judicial process." Yet another Senator objected to "positions taken by Justice Fortas since he went on the Supreme Court as Associate Justice [which had] reflected a view to the Constitution insufficiently rooted to the Constitution as it is written."[31] Opposition to Fortas was also based on money received for delivering university lectures while an Associate Justice and his close relationship and advisory role with President Johnson while an Associate Justice.

President Richard M. Nixon's nomination of Clement F. Haynsworth, Jr. in 1969 also failed partly on the basis of his perceived views. Like the Fortas

---

[28] For a description of the Parker nomination and a differing perspective on his record, see Harris, pp. 127-132. Abraham (pp. 42-43) also discusses the nomination and contests the claims offered by opponents.

[29] U.S. Congress, Committee on the Judiciary, Subcommittee, *Confirmation of Hon. J. Parker to be to be an Associate Justice of the Supreme Court of the United States*, hearings, 71st Cong., 2nd sess., April 5, 1930 (Washington: GPO, 1930), pp. 74-79.

[30] Ibid, pp. 23-60.

[31] All quotes from U.S. Congress, Senate Committee on the Judiciary, *Nomination of Abe Fortas*, report to accompany the nomination of Abe Fortas, 90th Cong., 2nd sess., Exec. Rept. 8 (Washington: GPO, 1968), pp. 15-44. See also Abraham, 43-45.

nomination, the Haynswrth nomination was reported favorably by the Committee in the Judiciary. In this case, the dissenting views in the committee's written report focused on perceived ethical lapses on the part of Judge Haynsworth. In addition, a joint statement by five Senators referred to "doubts about his record on the appellate bench," and one Senator opposed the nomination on the basis of the judge's record on civil rights issues.[32] Furthermore, Haynsworth drew criticism from labor and minority groups on the basis of his record. One historian has suggested that because of the recent rejection of Fortas on the basis of ethical questions, the ethical questions concerning Haynsworth played the largest role in his rejection.[33]

President Nixon's nomination of G. Harrold Carswell in 1970 was also opposed partly on the basis of his perceived views. The Committee on the Judiciary reported the nomination favorably with several dissenting views. One statement, issued jointly by four Senators, opposed the nomination in part because his "decisions and his courtroom demeanor [had] been openly hostile to the black, the poor, and the unpopular."[34] A more persistent theme in the dissent, however, was a perceived lack of competence and qualification for the position.[35]

Robert H. Bork, nominated by President Reagan in 1987, is the most recent Supreme Court nominee not to be confirmed by the Senate, as well as the most recent to be rejected on the basis of his views. Much has been written about this nomination, and it remains controversial. The Committee on the Judiciary reported the nomination unfavorably after 12 days of hearings. Although the written report raised some concerns about the nominee's evaluation by the American Bar Association and academic and legal communities and his role in the firing of Special Prosecutor Archibald Cox during the Nixon administration, the bulk of the report detailed concerns about and opposition to his publicly stated positions and judicial philosophy.[36]

---

[32] U.S. Congress, Senate Committee on the Judiciary, *Nomination of Clement F. Haynsworth, Jr.*, report to accompany the nomination of Clement F. Haynsworth, Jr., 91st Cong., 1st sess., Exec. Rept. 91-12 (Washington: GPO, 1969), pp. 24, 48.

[33] Abraham, pp. 14-15.

[34] U.S. Congress, Senate Committee on the Judiciary, *Nomination of George Harrold Carswell*, report to accompany the nomination of George Harrold Carswell, 91st Cong., 2nd sess., Exec. Rept. 91-14. (Washington: GPO, 1970), p. 13.

[35] Abraham, pp. 15-18.

[36] U.S. Congress, Senate Committee on the Judiciary, *Nomination of Robert H. Bork to be an Associate Justice of the United States Supreme Court,* 100th Cong, 1st sess., Exec. Rept. 100-7 (Washington: GPO, 1987).

Opposition to the Incumbent Court

The rejection by the Senate of a Supreme Court nominee on the basis of opposition to the incumbent Court is closely related to opposition on the basis of the nominee's views. In this case, the views and record of the incumbent Court majority are opposed, whereas the nominee is presumed to support the Court's views. In the case of Abe Fortas's nomination for Chief Justice, for example, the opposition of many Senators to the Warren Court has been cited as an influential factor. Fortas had been an Associate Justice for almost three yours at the time of his nomination, and some opposition hinged on his positions while on the Court, as discussed above. In addition, however, his elevation was opposed because of his affiliation with the Warren Court and its wider reputation. This opposition to the Warren Court in the context of the Fortas nomination is reflected in the individual views of a Senator in the committee report.[37] In addition, during the confirmation hearings, another Senator pointedly brought up a Warren Court opinion with which he disagreed, *Mallory v. United States,*[38] although, as he acknowledged, the case had preceded Fortas's appointment as Associate Justice by eight years.[39]

Senatorial Courtesy

At least seven Supreme Court nominations have failed to be confirmed partly on the basis of deference to the objections of the nominees' home-state Senators. New York's Senators objected to the nominations of Reuben H.Walworth by President Tyler.[40] President Polk's nomination of George W. Woodward of Pennsylvania was rejected, in part, due to the objection of one of the Senators from that state.[41] The last failed Supreme Court nominations that were attributed, in part, to senatorial courtesy came before the Senate in 1893-1894, when opposition by New York's Senators was instrumental in the failure of the nominations of William Hornblower and Wheeler H. Peckham, both also of New

[37] U.S. Congress, Senate Committee on the Judiciary, *Nomination of Abe Fortas*, report to accompany the nomination of Abe Fortas, 90th Cong., 2nd sess., Exec. Rept. 8 (Washington: GPO, 1968), pp. 20-30.

[38] 354 U.S. 449(1957). For the Senator's remarks, see U.S. Congress, Senate Committee on the Judiciary, *Nominations of Abe Fortas and Homer Thornberry,* hearings, 90th Cong., 1st sess., July 11, 12 16, 17, 18, 19, 20, 22, 23, 1968 (Washington: GPO, 1968), p. 191.

[39] Abraham, p. 44.

[40] Abraham, p. 27-28.

[41] Swindler, p. 538; Abraham, p. 41.

York.[42] No unsuccessful Supreme Court nomination since that time has been attributed to senatorial courtesy.[43]

Political Unreliability

One unsuccessful nominee was opposed in the Senate in part because of the perception that he was a "political chameleon."[44] One of President Grant's nominees for Chief Justice, Caleb Cushing, "had been, in turn, a regular Whig, a Tyler Whig, a Democrat, a[n Andrew] Johnson Constitutional Conservative, and finally a Republican."[45] The failure of his nomination has also been attributed to his advanced age (74) and a letter of introduction of a friend Cushing wrote to Confederate President Jefferson Davis in 1861.[46]

Lack of Qualification or Ability

As noted previously, President Madison's nomination of Alexander Wolcott[47] and President Nixon's nomination of G. Harrold Carswell[48] were opposed in part because of their perceived lack of qualification and ability. President Grant's nomination of George H. Williams faced similar opposition.[49] Williams also suffered from allegations of ethical misconduct.[50]

Interest Group Opposition

Interest groups were involved in confirmation fights as far back as 1881, when the Grange mounted a campaign in opposition to the Matthews

---

[42] Swindler, p. 541; Abraham, pp. 27-28.
[43] For a discussion of senatorial courtesy, see Harris, pp. 215-237.
[44] Abraham, p. 45. See also Harris, p. 76; Swindler pp. 540-541.
[45] Abraham, p. 45.
[46] Harris, p. 76; see also Jacobstein and Mersky, pp. 87-93 for a description of this nomination.
[47] Abraham, p. 41; Jacobstein and Mersky, pp. 14-17; Swindler, p. 535.
[48] Abraham 16-17. See also U.S. Congress, Senate Committee on the Judiciary, *Nomination of George Harrold Carswell,* report to accompany the nomination of George Harrold Carswell, 91st Cong., 2nd sess., Exec. Rept. 91-14 (Washington: GPO, 1970), pp. 13-17, 32-33, 36-38.
[49] Abraham, pp. 45-56; Harris, pp. 75-76.
[50] Jacobstein and Mersky, pp. 82-87.

nomination,[51] and they testified in opposition to (and, in some cases, support of) each of the Supreme Court nominations that were not confirmed in the twentieth century — Parker, Fortas, Thornberry, Haynsworth, Carswell, and Bork. The number of organized interest groups testifying at the confirmation hearings grew from two for the Parker nomination to more than twenty for the Bork nomination.[52] Interest groups have been active in unsuccessful Supreme Court confirmation processes in a number of other ways, as well, including conducting research on nominees' positions, lobbying Senators, providing information to the media, conducting television ad campaigns, sending mailings, and organizing constituent letters and calls.[53] Observers of the Supreme Court confirmation process have suggested that interest group opposition has not only grown, but has also been effective in preventing confirmations. The impact of interest group opposition relative to other factors is a matter of continuing study.[54]

Fear of Altering the Court

In addition to the above mentioned reasons for not confirming a nomination, the senate may fear altering the jurisprudential philosophy of the Court. In this case, opposition would be not only to the perceived views of the nominee, but also to the impact the nominee could have on the Court's ideological balance. The best-documented case where this factor appears to have been influential was President Reagan's nomination of Robert H. Bork. Bork was nominated to replace Associate Justice Lewis F. Powell, Jr., who had been the swing voter on an often evenly divided bench. If confirmed, Bork was expected to tip the Court to the

[51] John A. Maltese, *The Selling of Supreme Court Nominees* (Baltimore: The Johns Hopkins University Press, 1995), chapter 3.

[52] Maltese, chapter 6.

[53] Christine DeGregorio and Jack E. Rossoti, "Campaigning for the Court: Interest Group Participation in the Bork and Thomas Confirmation Process," in *Interest Group Politics,* 4th ed., Allan J. Cigler and Burdett A. Loomis, eds. (Washington: CQ Press, 1995), p. 215; and Gregory A. Caldeira, Marie Hojnacki, and John R. Wright, "The Lobbying Activities of Organized Interests in Federal Judicial Nominations" (paper presented at the 1996 Annual Meeting of the Midwest Political Science Association).

[54] See, for example, Jeffrey A. Segal, Charles M. Cameron, and Albert D. Cover, "A Spatial Model of Roll Call Voting: Senators, Constituents, Presidents, and Interest Groups in Supreme Court Confirmations," *Amerincan Journal of Political Science,* vol. 36, Feb. 1992, p. 96; and Gregory A. Caldeira and John R. Wright, "Lobbying for Justice: Organized Interests, Supreme Court Nominations, and the United States Senate," *American Journal of Political Science,* vol. 42, April 1998, p. 499.

conservative side, and some of the opposition to his nomination came from those who feared this change.[55]

The Committee on the Judiciary and Unsuccessful Nominations

Since 1816, the Senate has had a standing Committee on the Judiciary. Prior to that development, one of the three unsuccessful nominations had been referred to a select committee. Between 1816 and 1868, 11 of the 16 unsuccessful nominations had been referred to the Judiciary Committee. Since 1868, almost all Supreme Court nominations, including all that were ultimately not confirmed, have been automatically referred to the Judiciary Committee.[56]

Of the unsuccessful nominations that have been referred to the Judiciary Committee, four were never reported or discharged. The first three, Henry Stanbery, Stanley Matthews, and William Hornblower, are discussed above. The fourth was Homer Thornberry, nominated by President Lyndon B. Johnson to replace Justice Abe Fortas when he was nominated for elevation to Chief Justice. When Fortas's nomination was withdrawn by the President, the open position for Thornberry was effectively eliminated, and his nomination was also withdrawn. At that time, the nomination had not been reported by the Judiciary Committee.

Although their first nominations were never reported, second nominations of Matthews and Hornblower in subsequent sessions of Congress were reported to the full Senate. Only in the cases of Stanbery and Thornberry did nominations that had been referred to committee fail to be reported out of committee on any occasion; both of these nominations were associated with Associate Justice vacancies that ceased to exist while the nomination were pending.

Additional Information on Nominations

This report provides two additional tables of information concerning Supreme Court nominations. **Table 3** shows, by President, the number of vacancies, number of nominations, and disposition of nominations. **Table 4** provides detailed

---

[55] Abraham, 356-359; Jacobstein and Mersky, 160-170.

[56] U.S. Congress, Senate Committee on the Judiciary, *History of the Committee on the Judiciary, United States Senate, 1816-1981,* Senate Document no. 97-18, 97th Cong., 1st Sess. (Washington: GPO, 1982), p. iv.

information on the course and fate of each of the 32 unsuccessful Supreme Court nominations. A variety of sources were used to develop this table, as identified in the table notes. Although most of these sources are widely available, some, particularly older committee records, are located at the Notional Archives and Records Administration. Among the official sources, the *Journal of the Executive Proceedings of the Senate of the United States of America* and committee records, where available, provided the most information. Where the *Journal* showed no evidence of a debate or vote on the floor of the Senate, the indices of other official sources were also checked for evidence of any other Senate activity related to the nomination. These sources included the *Congressional Globe, Congressional Record, Annals of Congress,* and *Senate Journal.* Where the table indicates that there was no debate or further Senate action, there is no known official record that provides additional information. A list of related literature follows Table 4.

Table 3. Supreme Court Nominations by President

President (party)	Vacancies during Presidency[a]	Nominations	Confirmed and Served	Not Confirmed	Confirmed, and Declined or Died Prior to Service
Washington (Federalist)	10	14	10	2	2
J. Adams (Fed)	3	4	3	0	1
Jefferson (Democratic-Republican)	3	3	3	0	0
Madison (Dem-Rep)	2	5	2	1	2
Monroe (Dem-Rep)	1	1	1	0	0
J. Q. Adams (Dem-Rep)	2	2	1	1	0
Jackson (Democratic)	7	8	6	1	1
Van Buren (Dem)	2	2	2	0	0
W. H. Harrison (Whig)	0	0	0	0	0
Tyler (Whig)	2	9	1	8	0
Polk (Dem)	2	3	2	1	0
Tailor (Whig)	0	0	0	0	0
Fillmore (Whig)	2	4	1	3	0
Pierce (Dem)	1	1	1	0	0
Buchanan (Dem)	2	2	1	1	0

President (party)	Vacancies during Presidency[a]	Nominations	Confirmed and Served	Not Confirmed	Confirmed, and Declined or Died Prior to Service
Lincoln (Republican)	5	5	5	0	0
A. Johnson (Dem)	2[b]	1	0	1	0
Grant (Rep)	4	8	4	3	1
Hayes (Rep)	3	3	2	1	0
Garfield (Rep)	1	1	1	0	0
Arthur (Rep)	2	3	2	0	1
Cleveland (1) (Dem)	2	2	2	0	0
B. Harrison (Rep)	4	4	4	0	0
Cleveland (2) (Dem)	2	5	2	3	0
McKinley (Rep)	1	1	1	0	0
T. Roosevelt (Rep)	3	3	3	0	0
Taft (Rep)	6	6	6	0	0
Wilson (Dem)	3	3	3	0	0
Harding (Rep)	4	4	4	0	0
Coolidge (Rep)	1	1	1	0	0
Hoover (Rep)	3	4	3	1	0
F. D. Roosevelt (Dem)	9	9	9	0	0
Truman (Dem)	4	4	4	0	0
Eisenhower (Rep)	5	5	5	0	0
Kennedy (Dem)	2	2	2	0	0
L. B. Johnson (Dem)	4[c]	4	2	2	0
Nixon (Rep)	4	6	4	2	0
Ford (Rep)	1	1	1	0	0
Carter (Dem)	0	0	0	0	0
Reagan (Rep)	4	5	4	1	0
G. H. W. Bush (Rep)	2	2	2	0	0
Clinton (Dem)	2	2	2	0	0
Totals	122	152	112	32	8

[a] Includes unfilled vacancies remaining from previous administration; some vacancies are counted for more then one administration.

[b] Both positions were abolished, one until the Grant administration, the other permanently.

[c] One of these vacancies was the expected Associate Justice vacancy created when Johnson nominated Abe Fortas for elevation to Chief Justice. When the Fortas nomination was not successful, this expected vacancy ceased to exist.

Table 4. Supreme Court Nominations not Confirmed, 1789-2001

Nominee	President	Date nomination received in Senate[a]	Confirmation hearing date(s)[b]	Committee votes, reports, and recommendations	Date(s) of Senate debate	Final Disposition (vote)
William Paterson[c]	Washington	Feb. 27, 1793	Nomination predates standing Judiciary Committee; no record of other committee referral		No record of debate	Withdrawn, message received Feb. 28, 1793
John Rutledge (for Chief Justice)[d]	Washington	Dec. 10, 1975	Nomination predates standing Judiciary Committee; no record of other committee referral		Dec. 11, 15, 1795	Rejected (10-14), Dec. 15, 1795
Alexander Wolcott[e]	Madison	Feb. 4, 1811	Nomination predates standing Judiciary Committee on Feb. 7, 1811. The Committee reported on Feb. 13, 1811; no record of committee hearings, vote or recommendation		Feb. 5, 6, 7, 13, 1811	Rejected (9-24), Feb. 13, 1811
John J. Crittenden[f]	J.Q. Adams	Dec. 18, 1828 (referred)	No record of hearings	Reported on Jan. 26, 1829 with the recommendation that the Senate not act on the nomination during that session	Jan. 29, 30, 1829; Feb. 2, 3, 4, 5, 9, 12, 1829	Postponed[g] (23-17), Feb. 12, 1829
Roger B. Taney [h]	Jackson	Jan. 15, 1835	No record of referral to the Judiciary Committee		Jan. 20, 1835; Feb. 2, 1835; Mar. 3, 1835	Postponed indefinitely (24-21), Mar. 3, 1835
John C. Spencer[I]	Tyler	Jan. 9, 1844 (reffered)	No record of hearing	Reported on Jan. 30, 1844; no record of committee vote or recommendation	Jan. 31, 1844	Rejected (21-26), Jan. 31, 1844

Nominee	President	Date nomination received in Senate[a]	Confirmation hearing date(s)[b]	Committee votes, reports, and recommendations	Date(s) of Senate debate	Final Disposition (vote)
Reuben H. Walworht[k]	Tyler	Mar. 13, 1844 (reffered)	No record of hearings	Reported on June 14, 1844; no record of committee vote or recommendation	June 15, 1844	Tabled (27-20), June 15, 1844; withdrawn, message received June 17, 1844
Edward King[l]	Tyler	June 5, 1844 (reffered)	No record of hearings	Reported on June 14, 1844; no record of committee vote or recommendation	June 15, 1844	Tabled (29-18), June 15, 1844
John C. Spencer[m]	Tyler	June 17,1844 (withdrawn on the same day)	No record of referral to the Judiciary Committee		No record of debate on the nomination	Withdrawn, message received June 17, 1844
Reuben H. Walworth[n]	Tyler	June 17, 1844	No record of referral to the Judiciary Committee		Motion to consider the nomination was objected to, June 17, 1844	No record of further action
Reuben H. Walworth[o]	Tyler	Dec. 10, 1844 (referred)	No record of hearings	Reported on Jan. 21, 1845; no record of committee vote or recommendation	No record of debate	Tabled, Jan. 21, 1845 (no record of vote); withdrawn, message received Feb. 6, 1845

Nominee	President	Date nomination received in Senate[a]	Confirmation hearing date(s)[b]	Committee votes, reports, and recommendations	Date(s) of Senate debate	Final Disposition (vote)
Edward King[p]	Tyler	Dec. 10, 1844 (referred)	No record of hearings	Reported on Jan. 21, 1845; no record of committee vote or recommendation	No record of debate on the nomination	Tabled, Jan. 21, 1845 (no record of vote); withdrawn, message received Feb. 8, 1845
John M. Read[q]	Tyler	Feb. 8, 1845 (referred)	No record of hearings	Reported on Feb. 14, 1845; no record of committee vote or recommendation	Unsuccessful motion to consider nomination, Feb. 26, 1845	No further record of action
Geprge W. Woodward[r]	Polk	Dec. 23, 1845 (referred)	No record of hearings	Reported on Jan. 20, 1846; no record of committee vote or recommendation	Jan. 21, 22 1846	Rejected (20-29), Jan. 22, 1846
Edward A. Bradford[s]	Fillmore	Aug. 21, 1852 (referred)	No record of hearings	Reported on Aug. 30, 1852; no record of committee vote or recommendation	Aug. 31, 1852	Tabled Aug. 31, 1852 (no record of vote)
George E. Badger[t]	Fillmore	Jan. 10, 1853	No record of referral to the Judiciary Committee		Jan. 14, 20, 24, 1853; Feb. 7, 11, 1853	Postponed (26-25), Feb. 11, 1853
William Micou[u]	fillmore	Feb. 24, 1853 (referred and discharged on the same day)	No record of hearings	No record of committee vote; ordered discharged on Feb. 24, 1853, the same day as reffered	No record of debate	No record of action after discharge

Nominee	President	Date nomination received in Senate[a]	Confirmation hearing date(s)[b]	Committee votes, reports, and recommendations	Date(s) of Senate debate	Final Disposition (vote)
Jeremiah S. Black[v]	Buchanan	Feb. 6, 1861	No record of referral to the Judiciary Committee		Motions to consider the nomination unsuccessful, Feb. 6, 12, 21, 1861	No record of further action
Henry Stanbery[w]	A. Johnson	Apr. 16, 1866 (referred)	No record of hearings	No record of committee action[x]	No record of debate	No record of action after referral[y]
Ebenezer R. Hoar[z]	Grant	Dec. 15, 1869 (referred)	No record of hearings	Reported adversely on Dec. 22, 1869; no record of committee vote	Dec. 22, 1869, Feb. 3, 1870	Rejected (24-33), Feb. 3, 1870
George H. Williams (for Chief Justice)[aa]	Grant	Dec. 2, 1873 (referred Dec. 4, 1873)	Hearings held Dec. 16, 17, 1873 after recommittal	Reported favorably on Dec. 11, 1873; no record of committee vote Hearings held after recommittal; nomination withdrawn by the President; committee returned nomination to the Senate[bb]	Debated Dec. 11, 15, 1873; nomination recommitted to the Judiciary Committee, Dec. 15, 1873	Withdrawn, message received Jan. 8, 1874
Caleb Cushing (for chief Justice)[cc]	Grant	Jan. 9, 1874 (referred)	No record of hearings	Reported favorably on Jan. 9, 1874[dd]	No record of debate	Withdrawn, message received Jan. 14, 1874

Nominee	President	Date nomination received in Senate[a]	Confirmation hearing date(s)[b]	Committee votes, reports, and recommendations	Date(s) of Senate debate	Final Disposition (vote)
Stanley Matthews[ee]	Hayes	Jan. 26, 1881 (referred)	No record of hearings	Addressed on Feb. 7, 1881; addressed and postponed Feb. 14, 1881[ff]	No record of debate	No record of action after committee postponement[gg]
William B. Hornblower[hh]	Cleveland	Sept. 19, 1893 (referred)	No record of hearings	Addressed on Sept. 25, 1893; October 25, 30, 1893	No record of debate	No record of further action
William B. Hornblower	Cleveland	Dec. 6, 1893 (referred)	No record of hearings	Addressed on Dec. 11, 14, 18,1893; Reported adversely, Jan. 8, 1894[ii]	Jan. 15, 1894	Rejected (24-30) Jan. 15, 1894
Wheeler H. Peckham[jj]	Cleveland	Jan. 22, 1894 (referred)	No record of hearings	Addressed Jan. 29, 1894; Feb. 5, 6, 12, 1894; committee reportedly equally divided;[kk] reported without recommendation, Feb. 12, 1894	Feb. 15, 16, 1894	Rejected (32-41), Feb. 16, 1894
John J. Parker[ll]	Hoover	Mar. 21, 1930 (referred)	April 5, 1930[mm]	Reported adversely, April. 21, 1930[nn]	Apr. 28, 29, 30, 1930; May 1, 2, 5, 6, 7, 1930	Rejected (39-41), May 7, 1930

Nominee	President	Date nomination received in Senate[a]	Confirmation hearing date(s)[b]	Committee votes, reports, and recommendations	Date(s) of Senate debate	Final Disposition (vote)
Abe Fortas (for Chief Justice)[oo]	L. Johnson	June 26, 1968 (referred)	July 11, 12, 16, 17, 18, 19, 20, 22, 23, 1968; Sept. 13, 16, 1968[pp]	Committee voted to approve on Sept. 17, 1968[qq]; reported favorably on Sept. 20, 1968	Sept. 24, 25, 26, 27, 30, 1968; Oct. 1, 1968	Cloture motion defeated (45-43), Oct. 1, 1968; Withdrawn, message received Oct. 4, 1968
Homer Thornberry[rr]	L. Johnson	June 26, 1968 (referred)	July 11, 12, 16, 17, 18, 19, 20, 22, 23, 1968; Sept. 13, 16, 1968[ss]	No record of committee vote or report	No record of debate	Withdrawn message received Oct. 4, 1968[tt]
Clement F. Haynsworth, Jr.[uu]	Nixon	Aug. 18, 1969 (referred)	Sept. 16, 17, 18, 19, 23, 24, 25, 26, 1969[vv]	Committee voted 10-7 in favor of confirmation on Oct. 9, 1969[ww]; reported favorably on Nov. 12, 1969	Nov. 13, 14, 17, 18, 19, 20, 21, 1969	Rejected (45-55), Nov. 21, 1969
G. Harrold Carswell[xx]	Nixon	Jan. 19, 1970 (referred)	Jan. 27, 28, 29, 1970; Feb. 2, 3, 1970[yy]	Committee voted 13-4 in favor of recommending for confirmation on Feb. 16, 1970[zz]; reported on Feb. 27, 1970	Mar. 13, 16, 17, 18, 19, 20, 23, 24, 25, 26, 31, 1970; Apr, 3, 6, 7, 8, 1970	Rejected (45-51), Apr. 8, 1970
Robert H. Bork[aaa]	Reagan	July 7, 1987 (referred)	Sept. 15, 16, 17, 18, 19, 21, 22, 23, 25, 28, 29, 30, 1987[bbb]	5-9 against on Oct. 6, 1987; reported on Oct. 13, 1987[ccc]	Oct. 21, 22, 23 1987	Rejected (42-58), Oct. 23, 1987

[a] The date of the President's nomination and the date the nomination is received in the Senate are often, but not always, the same. As used in this column, "referred" indicates that the nomination was referred to the Senate Committee on the Judiciary on that date.

[b] The committee's deliberations were held in secret until the early twentieth century. CRS Report 94-497 GOV, *Senate Judiciary Committee Consideration of Supreme Court Nominations,* by Denis Steven Rutkus.

[c] Nomination information from U.S. Congress, Senate, *Journal of the Executive Proceedings of the Senate of the United States of America,* vol. 1, pp. 134-135. (Hereafter cited as nominee, *Executive Journal.)* Paterson was later nominated again and confirmed.

[d] Rutledge, *Executive Journal,* vol. 1, pp. 194-196. Rutledge served as Associate Justice from Feb. 15, 1790 through Mar. 5, 1791. Although Rutledge was never confirmed as chief Justice, he served in the position from Aug. 12, 1795 through Dec. 15, 1795 under a recess appointment by President Washington. (Members of the Supreme Court of he United States, " PDF document accessed at [http://www.supremecourtus.gov/about/about.html], visited Aug. 9, 2001.)

[e] Wolcott, *Executive Journal,* vol. 2, pp. 165-67.

[f] Crittenden, *Executive Journal,* vol. 3, pp. 622-623, 636-639, 643-644.

[g] Although the Senate did not take up a motion to "postpone indefinitely," as it did on other similar occasions, it passed a resolution which had the effect of postponing. (See Crittenden, *Executive Journal,* vol. 3, p. 644.)

[h] Taney, *Executive Journal,* vol. 4, pp. 459, 463, 465, 484. Taney was later nominated for Chief Justice and confirmed.

[i] Spencer was the subject of two nominations not confirmed. Information concerning the first nomination can be found at *Executive Journal,* vol. 6, pp. 207-208, 227, 229.

[j] In 1844 and 1845, President John Tyler forwarded nine nominations involving only five men. Eight of the nine were not confirmed. Of those nominees who were not confirmed, Walworth was nominated three times, Spencer and King were nominated twice, and Read was nominated once. Samuel Nelson was nominated once and confirmed.

[k] Walworth was the subject of three nominations not confirmed. Information concerning the first nomination can be found at *Executive Journal,* vol. 6, pp. 243-244, 332, 344-345, 353.

[l] King was the subject of two nominations not confirmed. Information concerning the first nomination can be found at *Executive Journal,* vol. 6, pp. 306, 332, 345.

[m] Spencer, *Executive Journal,* vol. 6, pp. 353-354.

[n] Walworth, *Executive Journal,* vol. 6, p. 354.

[o] Walworth, *Executive Journal,* vol. 6, pp. 355, 357, 387, 391.

[p] King, *Executive Journal,* vol. 6, pp. 355, 357, 387, 392.

[q] Read, *Executive Journal,* vol. 6, pp. 392, 396.

[r] Woodward, *Executive Journal,* vol. 7, pp. 10, 36-38.

[s] Bradford, *Executive Journal,* vol. 8, pp. 440-441, 448, 452.

[t] Badger, *Executive Journal,* vol. 9, pp. 10, 18-20, 26-28, 34. President Millard Fillmore indicated that he regarded the postponement of the Badger nomination as "equivalent to a rejection" in his message nominating William C. Micou (p. 34).

[u] Micou, *Executive Journal,* vol. 9, pp. 34-36.

[v] Black, *Executive Journal,* vol. 11, pp. 260-261, 271, 278.

[w] Stanbery, *Executive Journal,* vol. 15, part 1, pp. 720-721.

[x] Senate Judiciary Committee minutes are available for the session during which this nomination was pending. Specific information regarding this nomination or any other nomination, however, was not recorded. See U.S. Congress, Senate Committee on the Judiciary, "Senate Judiciary Committee, 39th–40th Congress, 1st sess.: Minutes," RG 46.15, U.S. National Archives.

[y] There in no record of action on this nomination. The Associate Justice position to which Stanbery was nominated was eliminated by statute after his nomination. He was nominated and confirmed for U.S. Attorney General in July 1866.

[z] Hoar, *Executive Journal,* vol. 17, pp. 314, 316, 328-330.

[aa] Williams, *Executive Journal,* vol. 19, pp. 119, 166, 183, 188-189, 210.

[bb] The date of this action is not specified in committee records. See U.S. Congress, Senate Committee on the Judiciary, "Papers are Nominations (P-W)," drawer Sen: 43B-A5 12, RG 46.15, U.S. National Archives.

[cc] Cushing, *Executive Journal,* vol. 19, pp. 212-213, 218.

[dd] The official vote of the committee is not reported. According to one press account, the committee was unanimous ("The Chief Justiceship," *New York Tribune,* Jan. 10, 1874, p. 1), while another reported a waiving of the formal referral of the nomination ("The Chief Justiceship," *New York Times,* Jan. 10, 1874, p. 1).

[ee] Matthews, *Executive Journal,* vol. 22, p. 469.

[ff] According to committee minutes, "The nomination of Stanly [sic] Matthews was taken up and on motion the further consideration of same was postponed until next Monday [Feb. 21, 1881]." The committee minutes contain no further report of action on the nomination during the remaining days of the 46th Congress. (U.S. Congress, Senate Committee on the Judiciary, *Senate Judiciary Committee 46th-48th Congress, 1st Session: Minutes,* pp. 53-54.)

[gg] Matthews was later nominated by President James A. Garfield and confirmed.

[hh] Hornblower was the subject of two nominations not confirmed. The first was at the end of the first session to the 53rd congress, and the second was at the beginning of the second session of the same Congress. *Executive Journal,* vol. 29, part 2, pp. 138, 142, 243, 251, 339, 352-353.

[ii] The official vote of the committee was not recorded. The *New York Times* reported the vote as 7-4 against ("Unfavorable to Mr. Hornblower," *New York Times,* Jan. 9, 1894, p. 1), and the *New York Tribune* reported 5-3 against ("To Reject Mr. Hornblower," *New York Tribune,* Jan. 9, 1894, p. 2).

[jj] Peckham, *Executive Journal,* vol. 29, part 2, pp. 356, 408, 421-423.

[kk] The official vote of the committee was not recorded. The *New York Times* reported the vote as 5-5 ("Peckham's Friends Hopeful," *New York Times,* Feb. 13, 1894, p. 1).

[ll] Parker, *Executive Journal,* vol. 69, part 1, pp. 525, 643, 655, 673, 682, 691, 695-696, 699, 705, 710, 718-722.

[mm] See U.S. Congress, Senate Committee on the Judiciary, *Confirmation of Hon. John J. Parker to be an Associate Justice of the Supreme Court of the United States,* hearings, 71st Cong, 2nd sess. (Washington: GPO, 1930).

[nn] The official committee vote was not reported in the *Executive Journal.* The *New York Times* reported a 10-6 vote against the nomination on Apr. 21, 1930 ("Committee, 10 to 6, Rejects Parker," *New York Times,* Apr. 22, 1930, pp. 1, 23). Another source provides a different vote count, 9-8, with the same outcome (Joseph P. Harris, *Advice and consent of the Senate; a Study* of *the Confirmation of Appointments* [New York: Greenwood Press, 1968], p.129).

[oo] Fortas, *Executive Journal,* vol. 110,. pp. 332, 516, 521, 527, 529, 554-556, 569-570, 592.

[pp] U.S. Congress, Senate Committee on the Judiciary, *Nomination of Abe Fortas,* report to accompany the nomination of Abe Fortas, 90th Cong., 2nd sess., Exec. Rept. 8 (Washington: GPO, 1968). See also U.S. Congress, Senate Committee on the Judiciary, *Nominations of Abe Fortas and Homer Thornberry,* hearings, 90th Cong., 2nd sess. (Washington: GPO, 1968).

[qq] The official committee vote was not reported in the *Executive Journal.* The *New York Times* reported an 11-6 vote in favor of the nomination on Sept. 17, 1968 ("Fortas Approved by Senate Panel; Filibuster Looms," *New York Times,* Sept. 18, 1968, pp. 1, 13).

[rr] Thornberry, *Executive Journal,* vol. 110, pp. 332, 592.

[ss] The Thornberry hearings were conducted in conjunction with the Fortas hearings. See U.S. Congress, Senate Committee on the Judiciary, *Nominations of Abe Fortas and Homer Thornberry,* hearings, 90th Cong., 2nd sess. (Washington: GPO, 1968).

[tt] With the nomination of Abe Fortas to be Chief Justice withdrawn, there was no longer an Associate Justice vacancy.

[uu] Haynsworth, *Executive Journal,* vol. pp. 590, 768-770.772-773, 776.

[vv] See U.S. Congress, Senate Committee on the Judiciary, *Nomination of Clement F. Haynswoth, Jr.,* hearings, 91st Cong., 1st sess. (Washington: GPO, 1969).

[ww] Vote Tally from U.S. Congress, Senate Committee on the Judiciary, *Nomination of Clement F. Haynsworth, Jr.*, report to accompany the nomination of Clement F. Haynsworth, Jr., 91st Cong., 1st sess., Exec. Rept. 91-12 (Washington: GPO, 1969): date of vote from U.S. Congress, Senate Committee on the Judiciary, *Legislative and Executive Calendar,* 91st Cong., 1st and 2nd sess. (Washington: GPO, 1970), p. 434.

[xx] Carswell, *Executive Journal,* vol. 112, pp. 1, 79, 117, 121, 125, 127-130, 139-141, 144-148.

[yy] See U.S. Congress, Senate Committee on the Judiciary, *George Harrold Carswell,* hearings, 91st Cong., 2nd sess. (Washington: GPO, 1970).

[zz] Vote tally from U.S. Congress, Senate Committee on the Judiciary, *Nomination of George Harrold Carswell*, report to accompany the nomination of George Harrold Carswell, 91st Cong., 2nd sess., Exec. Rept. 91-14 (Washington: GPO, 1970); date of vote from U.S. Congress, Senate Committee on the Judiciary, *Legislative and Executive Calendar,* 91st Cong., 1st and 2nd sess. (Washington: GPO, 1970), p. 442.

[aaa] Bork, *Executive Journal,* vol. 129, pp. 493, 665, 669-771.

[bbb] See U.S. Congress, Senate Committee on the Judiciary, *Nomination of Robert H. Bork to be Associate Justice of the Supreme Court of the United States,* hearings, 5 parts, 100th Cong., 1st sess. (Washington: GPO, 1987).

[ccc] U.S. Congress, Senate Committee on the Judiciary, *Legislative and Executive Calendar,* S.Prt. 100-153, 100th Cong., 1st and 2nd sess. (Washington: GPO, 1989). See also U.S. Congress, Senate Committee on the Judiciary, *Nomination of Robert H. Bork to be an Associate Justice of the United States Supreme Court,* report to accompany the nomination of Robert H. Bork, 100th Cong., 1st sess., Exec. Rept. 100-7 (Washington: GPO, 1987).

ADDITIONAL RESOURCES

Abraham, Henry J., Justices, Presidents, and Senators: A History of the U.S. Supreme Court Appointments from Washington to Clinton, 4th ed. (Lanham, MD: Rowman & Littlefield, 1999).

Ginsburg, Ruth Bader, "Confirming Supreme Court Justices; Thoughts on the Second Opinion Rendered by the Senate," University of Illinois Law Review, vol 1988, pp. 101-117.

Harris, Joseph P., The Advice and Consent of the Senate: A Study of the Confirmation of Appointments by the United States Senate (New York: Greenwood Press, 1968).

Jacobstein, J. Myron, and Roy M. Mersky, The Rejected: Sketches of the 26 Men Nominated for the Supreme Court but Not Confirmed by the Senate (Milpitas, CA: Toucan Valley Publications, 1993). [The authors do not include the Paterson nomination.]

Maltese, John Anthony, The Selling of Supreme Court Nominees (Baltimore: The Johns Hopkins University Press, 1995).

Massaro, John, Supremely Political: The Role of Ideology and Presidential Management in Unsuccessful Supreme Court Nominations (Albany, NY: State University of New York Press, 1990).

Massey, Calvin R., "Getting There: A Brief History of the Politics of Supreme Court Appointments," Hastings Constitutional Law Quarterly, vol. 19, Fall 1991, pp. 1-21.

Sulfridge, Wayne, "Ideology as a Factor in Senate Consideration of Supreme Court Nominations," The Journal of Politics, vol. 42, no. 2, May 1980, pp. 560-567.

Thorpe, James A., "The Appearance of Supreme Court Nominees Before the Senate Judiciary Committee," in The First Branch of American Government: the United States Congress and Its Relations to the Executive and Judiciary, 1789-1989, vol. 2, Joel Sibley, ed. (Brooklyn, NY: Carlson, 1991) pp. 515-546.

Tulis, Jeffrey K., "The Appointment Power: Constitutional Abdication: The Senate, the President, and Appointments to the Supreme Court," Case Western Reserve Law Review, vol. 47, Summer 1997, pp. 1331-1357.

Chapter 2

THE SUPREME COURT APPOINTMENT PROCESS: SHOULD IT BE REFORMED?

Denis Steven Rutkus

INTRODUCTION

When the U.S. Senate on October 15, 1991 voted 52 to 48 to confirm the nomination of Clarence Thomas of Georgia to be an Associate Justice on the Supreme Court, it marked the culmination of an appointment process that had been remarkable for its controversy and contentiousness.

That process had begun three and a half months earlier, on June 27, 1991, when Justice Thurgood Marshall, 82, announced his intention to retire from the Supreme Court, followed on July 1 by the announcement of President George Bush of his intention to nominate a 43-year-old U.S. appellate court judge, Clarence Thomas, to replace Justice Marshall.[1]

The highly controversial nature of the Thomas nomination was reflected in the following weeks and months by unusual procedural actions taken both at the committee and the Senate floor level. These actions included:

---

[1] For a concise chronology of the Thomas nomination and confirmation process, along with discussion of major issuers surrounding the Thomas nomination, see U.S. Library of Congress. Congressional Research Service. *Major Legislation of the Congress; Summary Issue/102d Congress/November 1992*. Washington, 1992. pp. MLC-051 & MLC-052.

- a first set of confirmation hearings in September 1991 at which the nominee was questioned by the Senate Judiciary Committee for five consecutive hearing days (equalling a record set in 1987 by hearings on Supreme Court nominee Robert H. Bork);[2]
- a rare, although not unprecedented, committee vote to report the nomination to the full Senate without a favorable recommendation; [3]
- a last-minute delay by the Senate in its scheduled floor vote on the Thomas nomination, to allow the Judiciary Committee time to conduct a second set of hearings — this time into newly disclosed allegations that the nominee had once engaged in sexual harassment of a professional colleague;[4]
- a second set of Judiciary Committee hearings, televised live and viewed by millions of Americans, at which law professor Anita Hill testified in detail regarding her sexual harassment allegations, after which Judge Thomas testified and categorically denied the allegations;[5] and,

---

[2] Judge Thomas testified before the Committee on September 10, 11, 12, 13, and 16, 1991, followed by three more days of hearings, on September 17, 19, and 20, for other witnesses testifying in support of or against the nomination. Prior to this, Judge Bork in 1987 (whose nomination eventually was rejected by the full Senate), was the only Supreme Court nominee ever to have spent five days before the Judiciary Committee. See Biskupic, Joan. Thomas Hearings Illustrate Politics of the Process. *Congressional Quarterly Weekly Report,* v. 49, September 21, 1991. pp. 2688-92; U.S. Congress. Senate. Committee on the Judiciary. *Nomination of Robert H. Bork To Be Associate Justice of the Supreme Court of the United States.* Hearings, 100th Cong., 1st Sess., Part 1, Sept. 15-30, 1987. Washington, U.S. Govt. Print. Off., 1989. pp. 1-864.

[3] On September 27, 1991, a motion in the Judiciary Committee to recommend that the Senate confirm the Thomas nomination failed by a tie vote of 7 to 7. The Committee then voted 13 to 1 to report the Thomas nomination with no recommendation. See Marcus, Ruth. Divided Committee Refuses To Endorse Judge Thomas. *Washington Post,* September 28, 1991. pp A1,A6.
In two other instances in this century, the Judiciary Committee reported out a Supreme Court nomination other than favorably, each time with a recommendation that the nomination *be rejected.* The two nominations reported adversely were those of John J. Parker in 1930 and Robert H. Bork in 1987. Both nominations subsequently were rejected by the Senate. See (for Parker) U.S. Congress. Senate. *Journal of the Executive Proceedings of the Senate of the United States of America.* Volume 49, Part 1, 71st Cong., 2d Sess., from December 2, 1929 to July 3, 1930. Washington, U.S. Govt. Print. Off., 1959. p. 643; and (for Bork) U.S. Congress. Senate. Committee on the Judiciary, *Nomination of Robert H. Bork to be an Associate Justice of the United States Supreme Court.* Report. Executive Report 100-7, 100th Cong., 1st Sess. Washington, U.S. Govt. Print Off., 1987. 407p.; see also Walsh, Edward, and Al Kamen. Senate Panel Votes 9-5 To Reject Bork. *Washington Post*, October 7, 1987. pp. A1, A14.

[4] See U.S. Congress. Senate. Unanimous-Consent Agreement. *Congressional Record*, Daily Edition, v. 137, October 8, 1991. p. S14565-71; Glasser, Susan B. In Thomas Uproar, Rules Become Focus of Hot Debate in Both House and Senate. *Roll Call*, v. 37, October 10, 1991. p. 18.

[5] See Biskupic, Joan. Thomas Drama Engulfs Nation; Anguished Senate Faces Vote. *Congressional Quarterly Weekly Report*, v. 49, October 12, 1991. pp. 2948-57.

- a closing debate on the nomination by the full Senate, which, although culminating in a vote to confirm, included 48 nays — the most votes ever cast against a nominee confirmed to the Court.[6]

Although principally concerned with the issue of whether the nominee should be confirmed, the Thomas confirmation battle also focused the attention of Congress on other issues as well. One was the problem of sexual harassment of women in the workplace and whether existing legal protection against such harassment was adequate.[7] Related to this was the question of whether the predominantly male composition of Congress caused it to be insensitive to the problem of sexual harassment and to other issues involving the rights of women.[8]

The Thomas confirmation struggle also focused the attention of the Senate on perceived imperfections in the Supreme Court appointment process. In Congress, the news media, and academia, many asserted that the appointment process had become too partisan and ideologically divisive, and that the battle between those favoring and those opposing the confirmation of Judge Thomas has been waged with such stuidency as to shake public confidence in the Senate.[9]

During the final hours of Senate debate on the Thomas nomination, Senator Mark O. Hatfield (R-OR) was among those who called for reform, declaring:

---

[6] See U.S. Congress. Senate. Executive Session; Nomination of Clarence Thomas, of Georgia, To Be An Associate Justice of the Supreme Court of the United States. *Congressional Record*, Daily Edition, v. 137, October 15, 1991. pp S14626-705.

[7] See Jordan, Mary, and Stephen Buckley. In the Workplace, Closing Mouths and Opening Minds. *Washington Post,* October 20, 1991. pp. A1, A23; Claymer, Adam. Some See Lever for Rights Bill in What senators Said About Harassment. *New York Times*, October 21, 1991. p. A14. See also US. Library of Congress. Congressional Research Service. *Sexual Harassment in the Workplace: Selected References*. Report No. 91-836 L, by Jean Bowers. Washington, 1991. 7 p.

[8] This question had become a matter of controversy during the second set of hearings on the Thomas nomination, when the 14 Members of the Senate Judiciary Committee, all men, heard the testimony of a female law professor, Anita Hill, accusing a male Supreme Court nominee, Clarence Thomas, of sexual harassment, and the testimony of the latter denying those accusations. Some outside observers maintained that overall the Committee's questioning of the nominee and the witness was biased in favor of Judge Thomas, reflecting the fact that none of the Committee's Members had a female perspective. The full senate would also be accused of largely being, by virtue of its 98% male composition, unsympathetic to Professor Hill's allegations and insensitive to the problem of sexual harassment. See: Schwartz, Maralee. Feminists Vow To Seek Political Changes. *Washington Post*, October 17, 1991. p. A7; Marcus, Ruth, and Dan Balz. Committee Falls Short of Biden's Stated Goal. *Washington Post*, October 15, 1991. pp. A1, A6. Berke, Richard L. Thomad Hearings May Be Over, But Senators Find a War Looming. *New York Times*, October 25, 1991. p. A14. See also Resnik, Judith. Hearing Women. *Southern California Law Review*, v. 65, March 1992. pp. 1333-45.

[9] See, e.g., Biskupic, Joan. A process Under Scrutiny. *Congressional Quarterly Weekly Report,* v. 49, October 19, 1991. p. 3031 (hereafter cited as Biskupic, Process Under Scrutiny); Garrett, Major. Hearings Scar Image of Senate. *Washington Times*, October 20, 1991. pp. A1, A6; Balz, Dan. Thomas Hearings Resonate Across U.S. *Washington Post*, October 17, 1991. pp. A1, A10.

> ...the casualties of the Senate confirmation process continue to pile up like so many casualties of war. Nominees and witnesses alike wither under the white hot glare of the media spotlight and the searching beam of secret background checks. Once sterling reputations are clumsily smudged with the dingy tarnish of crude innuendo. This body must take action to stop what is now becoming commonplace in our confirmation process. We must have no more political casualties in the judicial confirmation process.[10]

Shortly thereafter, during the same debate, Senate Majority Leader George J. Mitchell (D-ME) also faulted the confirmation process for having become too politicized:

> ...the confirmation process has become uncomfortable and demeaning for all concerned. It has taken on the trappings of a political campaign. Indeed, in the eyes of many Americans, the process has become confused with electoral politics. It must be changed.[11]

The Thomas confirmation battle and its aftermath generated numerous proposals to reform the Supreme Court appointment process. Proposals of various kinds were advanced by Members of Congress, legal scholars, political scientists, news media commentators, and other observers. The following pages review and examine many of these proposals, providing background on the concerns which gave rise to each and the arguments that have been made or implied in support of, or against, their adoption. The examination also covers changes which actually have been implemented since the Senate confirmed the Thomas nomination.

Examined are specific proposals or actions taken as they relate to five general aspects of the Supreme Court appointment process: (1) the President's selection of a nominee; (2) the Senate Judiciary Committee's investigation of the nominee; (3) the involvement of outside interest groups; (4) the Senate's decision whether to confirm or reject; and, (5) the overall length of the nomination and confirmation process.

Also provided, in an Appendix, is a chronology of notable events pertaining to the Supreme Court appointment process which have occurred since the Senate's October 15, 1991 confirmation of Judge Thomas.

---

[10] Hatfield, Mark O. Nomination of Clarence Thomas, of Georgia, To Be An Associate Justice of the Supreme Court of the United States. Remarks in the Senate. *Congressional Record*, Daily Edition, v. 137, October 15, 1991. p. S14693.

[11] Mitchell, George J. Nomination of Clarence Thomas, of Georgia, To be An Associate Justice of the Supreme Court of the United States. Remarks in the Senate. *Congressional Record*, Daily Edition, v. 137, October 15, 1991. p. S14703.

In the following pages, it should be stressed, the phrase "appointment process" is used in the broadest sense — to include both the President's selection of a nominee (the "nomination process") and the Senate's deliberations and decision on whether to; confirm the nominee (the "confirmation process").

AN OVERVIEW OF RECENT PROPOSALS FOR CHANGE

Presidential Selection of a Nominee

President Bush's nomination of Clarence Thomas served, among other things, to draw attention to the process by which Presidents select Supreme Court nominees. Subsequently, several different proposals were offered which would alter the selection process. The proposed changes would affect four aspects of the process in particular: the role of the Senate in advising the President on his selection; the degree of openness in the selection process; the executive's investigation of a prospective nominee; and the criteria used by the President in choosing a nominee.

Senate's Advisory Role

Numerous critics of the Supreme Court nomination process have proposed that the Senate perform a more active role in advising the President before he selects his nominee. One such proposal was offered in the form of a Senate resolution on October 15, 1991, the day the Senate voted to confirm Clarence Thomas as an Associate Justice. Sponsored by a member of the Judiciary Committee, Senator Paul Simon (D-IL), S. Res. 194 as introduced expressed the sense of the Senate that "there should be informal, bipartisan consultation with some Members of the Senate on who is to be named to the Supreme Court before a name is submitted to the Senate."[12] That the president receive advice from the Senate, in Senator Simon's view, was especially important with respect to judicial nominations:

> Unlike the President's nominations to positions in the executive branch, appointments to the judiciary are to a branch of Government that is supposed

---

[12] Senate Resolution 194 – Relative to Appointments to the United States Supreme Court. *Congressional Record,* Daily Edition, v. 137, October 15, 1991. pp. S14712-13. When the 102d Congress adjourned sine die on October 8, 1992, no senate action had been taken on S. Res. 194.

> to be independent of the President. What is more, these appointments will serve a lifetime, and can only be removed by impeachment. For the President to control such appointments unilaterally would be inappropriate, especially in a political system where checks and balances are so important.[13] (Emphasis added)

A call for consultation between the Senate and the President also came from the Senate Democratic Task Force on the Confirmation Process, which had been appointed by the Senate Majority Leader in October 1991 to examine the confirmation process. In its December 1991 report, the Task Force recommended that there be consultation between the Senate and the President even before the next vacancy occurred on the Supreme. Court. "*Immediate* consultations between the President and Senate leaders on future Supreme Court nominations should *now* begin," the Task force urged.[14] (Emphasis added)

President Bush spoke both positively and negatively about the idea of accepting more input from the Senate before choosing his nominees. In remarks to a public gathering shortly after the Senate confirmed the Thomas nomination, the President maintained that "we have worked hard to cooperate with Congress and we welcome closer consultation." However, he then added:

> But let me make it clear: I will not give a group of senators veto power over a nominee before the Senate has conducted hearings and held a confirmation vote. I will not surrender presidential authority or powers any more than Congress will surrender its power.[15]

Not ruling out recommendations from Senators, the President clearly reserved for himself the option of rejecting any such recommendations and selecting as a nominee even one opposed in advance by consulting Senators. The president did not address the issue of whether he should begin accepting input from the Senate immediately, in anticipation of the next vacancy on the Supreme Court; this issue

---

[13] Simon, Paul. Taking Advice and Consent Seriously. Remarks in the Senate. *Congressional Record*, Daily Edition, v. 138, February 7, 1992. p. S1508.

[14] Report of the Task Force on the Confirmation Process (U.S. Senate, December 18, 1991). *Congressional Record*, Daily Edition, v. 138, February 4, 1992. pp. S897-98. (Hereafter cited as Democratic Task Force, Report) The task force was chaired by Senator Wendell H. Ford of Kentucky, Democratic Chairman of the Rules and Administration Committee. The task force's other four members were: Senator Joseph R.. Biden, Jr., of Delaware, Chairman of the Judiciary Committee; Senator David L. Boren of Oklahoma, Chairman of the Select Committee on Intelligence; Senator Sam Nunn of Georgia, Chairman of the Armed Services Committee; and Senator Claiborne Pell of Rhode Island, Chairman of the Foreign Relations Committee.

[15] U.S. President, 1989-93(Bush) Remarks to Representatives of Public Administration Groups on Public Service, October 24, 1991. *Weekly Compilation of Presidential Documents*, v. 27, October 28, 1991. p. 1497. (Hereafter cited as Bush, Remarks to Public Administration Groups)

materialized later, with the release of the report of the Senate Democratic Task Force report on February 4, 1992.

While the President declined to comment on the report, Senate Minority Leader Bob Dole (R KS) derided the Task Force proposal for immediate consultations between the President and Senate leaders. Senator Dole commented:

> When the Democrats suggest that the President immediately begin consulting with the Democratic Senate about the next Supreme Court nominee — at a time there is no vacancy on the Court — they are dreaming of a world that never was and never will be. This is nothing more than a blatant attempt to grab power which the Senate has never had.[16]

In Senator Dole's view, the "plain language of the Constitution... excludes the Senate from the nomination process and only involves the Senate in the appointment process." The President would be "surrendering" the nomination power to the Senate if he agreed to the Task force proposal, Senator Dole maintained.[17]

Notwithstanding Senator Dole's remarks, the Chairman of the Judiciary Committee, Senator Joseph R. Biden, Jr. (D-DE), issued his own call "for more Executive-Senate consultations." On June 25, 1982, in an extended Senate floor speech on the confirmation process, Senator Biden maintained that within the Bush administration the process of selecting Supreme Court nominees "has become dominated by the right[,] intent on using the Court to implement an ultraconservative social agenda that the Congress and the public have rejected." In light if this, Senator Biden said,

> I can have only one response. . . . Either we must have a compromise in the selection of future Justices or I must oppose those who are a product of this ideological nominating process, as is the right of others to conclude they should support nominees who are a product of this process.
>
> Put another way, if the President does not restore the historical tradition of genuine consultation between the White House and the Senate on the Supreme Court nomination, or instead restore the common practice of Presidents who chose nominees who strode the middle ground between the

---

[16] Dole, Bob. Democratic Report on the Nominations Process. Remarks in the Senate. *Congressional Record,* Daily Edition, v. 138, February 7, 1992. p. S1308.

[17] *Ibid.*

> divided political branches, then I shall oppose his future nominees immediately upon their nomination.[18]

Senator Biden rejected the idea that he was asking the president to relinquish any power to the Senate, "or that he refrain from exercising any prerogatives he has as President. Rather, it is my statement that unless the President *chooses* to do so, I will not lend the power that I have in this process to support the confirmation of his selection."[19] (Emphasis added)

The position laid out by Senator Biden in turn was faulted by the Ranking Minority Member on the Judiciary Committee, Senator Strom Thurmond (R-SC). In a floor statement, Senator Thurmond declared that the "net result of Senator Biden's recommendation would require President Bush, or any President, to seek and obtain the approval of a small but vocal minority of Senators and special interest groups who have failed to defeat his previous nominees. "Nothing that some Presidents in the past had consulted with Members of Congress and party leaders "prior to the actual nomination," Senator Thurmond maintained that this practice, while "understandable," was "clearly not mandated" by the Constitution.[20]

Criteria Used by President in Making Selection

Another type of reform would congressionally urge, if not require, the President to use specified criteria in determining whom to nominate to the

---

[18] Biden, Joseph R., Jr. Reform of the Confirmation Process. Remarks in the Senate. *Congressional Record*, Daily Edition, v. 138, June 25, 1992. p. S8863. (Hereafter cited as Biden, Reform of Confirmation Process)

[19] *Ibid*. Senator Biden stressed that consultation or compromise between the White House and Senate on Supreme Court nominations is essential whenever a President is faced with "a philosophically differing Senate." Hence, if, in the November 1992 general elections, the Democratic Party gained control of the White House and the Republicans became the new majority party in the Senate, Senator Biden said he would call upon the new President (as he already had called upon George Bush) to consult with the Senate on Supreme Court nominations: "...I will say the same thing to Bill Clinton: In a divided Government, he must seek the advice of the Republican Senate and compromise. Otherwise this Republican Senate Would be totally entitled to say we reject the nominees of a Democratic President who is attempting to remake the Court in a way with which we disagree." *Ibid*., p. S8864.

[20] Thurmond, Strom. Response to Senator Biden's Remarks on the Confirmation Process of Supreme Court Nominees. *Congressional Record,* Daily Edition, v. 138, June 25, 1992. p. S8867. See also the remarks of Senator Charles Grassley of Iowa, another member of the Judiciary Committee, in which he comments critically on the belief of "many Members of this body that the President must compromise his choice of a nominee with various Senators." Grassley, Charles. The Nomination Process. Remarks in the Senate. *Congressional Record,* Daily Edition, v. 138, July 2, 1992. p. S9574.

Supreme Court. Advocates of this approach have argued that a nominee — especially when here are deep political divisions between a President and a Senate majority — should be chosen for reasons other than whether the appointment would advance the President's political philosophy and agenda. In this vein, Senator Biden said during the Committee's first set of hearings on the Supreme Court nomination of Clarence Thomas: "I yearn for the day... when the President, Democrat or Republican, picks a nominee simply based upon their overall instinct about what their intellectual capacity is and not what their views are.[21]

One resolution introduced in the 102d Congress, S, Res. 194, sought to underscore to the President the importance of having "philosophical balance" on the Court. Sponsored by Senator Simon, a Member of the judiciary Committee, the resolution expressed the sense of the Senate that

> ...the President, in determining whom to name to any future Supreme Court vacancies, should keep philosophical in mind, so that the law in not like a pendulum, swinging back and forth depending upon the philosophy of the President.[22]

Expressing the same concern, Guido Calabresi, Dean of the Yale Law School, has urged that when Presidents of the same party have controlled the White House for a long period, they should, for the sake of diversity, deliberately nominate Justices from the other political party.[23]

Senator Biden, in a June 15, 1992 Senate speech, noted that the Republican Party had controlled the White House for 20 of the last 24 years, while the Democrats had controlled the Senate for 18 years of this period. "The public," he said, "has not given either party a mandate to remake the Court into a body reflective of our respective philosophies, and both of our parties should finally, honestly admit to that fact." The Senator cited approvingly the example set by Presidents Hoover, Eisenhower and Nixon. In the face of a Senate controlled by the opposition party or by a majority with a differing political philosophy than his

---

[21] Biskupic, Joan. Thomas Hearings Illustrate politics of the Process. *Congressional Quarterly Weekly Report,* v. 49, September 21, 1991. p. 2689. (Hereafter cited as Biskupic, Thomas Hearings Illustrate Politics) Senator Biden continued: "I doubt whether there is a single American out there who believes that President Bush said, 'By the way, just go find me a nominee who has an open mind, just find me nominee who has integrity, just find me nominee who is schooled in the law; I ask no more.'" *Ibid.*

[22] Senate Resolution 194 – Relative to Appointments to the United States Supreme Court. *Congressional Record,* Daily Edition, v. 137, October 15, 1991. pp. S14712-13. Subsequently, during the remainder of the 102d Congress, no Senate committee or floor action was taken on this resolution.

[23] Biskupic, Thomas Hearings Illustrate Politics, P. 2689.

own, each of these Presidents, according to Senator Biden," "consulted with the Senate about their choices for the Court and/or *chose nominees with balanced or diverse ideologies.*"[24] (Emphasis added)

Others, however, have expressed the view that a President may properly base his selection of a Supreme Court nominee on whether the appointment would advance his political agenda — provided the nominee also meets standards of legal qualification, ethical background, and judicial temperament. Senator Dole has told Senate colleagues that Presidential nominations of judges "traditionally have reflected Presidential agendas." He added:

> Any precept that a President should not use the appointment process to promote political objectives, or avert their subversion, is irrational and to the extent that it fosters expectations of executive forbearance, is also unrealistic.[25]

In a similar vein, Senator Charles E. Grassley (R-IA), another member of the Judiciary Committee, has characterized as "remarkable" and having "no historical basis" the "notion that President should consider balance on the Court in selecting his nominees." Senator Grassley pointed to the Supreme Court nominations of presidents Franklin D. Roosevelt and Lyndon B. Johnson:

> As an example, Franklin Roosevelt did not consider balance when he made his seventh and eighth nominations to the Supreme Court. Lyndon Johnson did not consider balance when he named Justices to what was already the most ideologically monolithic Court in the history of our country. Few, if anyone, suggested that Presidents Johnson or Franklin Roosevelt should have.[26]

---

[24] Biden, Reform of Confirmation Process, p. S8854. "Even President Nixon, who showed no reluctance to take full advantage of Presidential prerogatives, balanced his choice of conservatives Warren Burger and William Rehnquist with those of moderate Republican Harry Blackmun and conservative Democrat Lewis Powell." *Ibid.*

[25] Dole, Bob. Democratic Report on the Nominations Process. Remarks in the Senate. *Congressional Record,* Daily Edition, v. 138, February 7, 1992. p. S1308. Earlier in these remarks Senator Dole pointed to history to support his position. He noted that "President Washington… filled the Court with staunch supporters of a strong Federal Government," while John Adams "likewise sought to appoint Justices with strong federalist sentiments… ." Similarly, Senator Dole continued, it "was Franklin Roosevelt's objective to fashion a Court sympathetic to New Deal legislation." *Ibid.*, p. S1307.

[26] Grassley, Charles, The nomination Process. Remarks in the Senate. *Congressional Record,* Daily Edition, v. 138, July 2, 1992. p. S9574.

Degree of Openness in the Selection Process

Discussions of the Supreme Court appointment process have also focused on the ordinarily closed process by which the President selects a nominee to the Court. For example, Senator Dennis DeConcini (D-AZ.), a member of the senate Judiciary Committee, has observed:

> Unfortunately, we never witness the President's examination of the nominee's suitability and qualifications in the broad sense. The American public has no idea what political or ideological screening or questioning is conducted during the executive branch's review of a potential nominee. Because the President's evaluation is hidden from public inspection, the public's perception of the Senate's portion of the process is increased.[27]

Accordingly, a number of observers have advocated opening up, and making more public, the process by which the President selects a Supreme Court nominee. To do so, it has been argued, would decrease the influence of political considerations and make legal qualifications a more important factor in the President's selection.

Under one proposal the President would assemble a list of approximately five prospects and submit these names to the Senate, not for confirmation initially, but for advice. The list would be made public "so that all of us can know what is going on and can aid in the investigation and the giving of advice."[28] Receiving advice from the Senate regarding the listed individuals, the President would then narrow the selection "to at least one mutually acceptable, highly competent nominee, thereby reflecting substantial national consensus from the very beginning."[29]

A more open selection process almost certainly would increase the role played by the Senate and the press in evaluating prospective nominees. In a scenario described by one reform proponent, each of the President's announced "candidates" for the Court would be scrutinized not only by the Federal Bureau of Investigation and the American Bar Association but also by Senate investigators

---

[27] DeConcine, Dennis. Examining the Judicial Nomination Process: The Politics of Advice and Consent. *Arizona Law Review,* v. 34, 1992. p. 5. (Hereafter cited as DeConcini, Examining the Process)

[28] Forrester, Ray. A Call for integrity. *Hastings Constitutional Law Quarterly,* v. 19, Fall 1991. p. 18. (Hereafter cited as Forrester, Call for Integrity) The author is identified by this article as Professor of Constitutional Law, University of California, Hastings College of the Law.

[29] *Ibid.*, p. 19. See also Tofel, Richard. Four Steps to Better Hearings. *Legal Times,* v. 14, October 21, 1991. p. 22. (Hereafter cited as Tofel, Four Steps). Tofel maintains that a President "would be well-served if the White House publicly announced a list of three to five candidates from which the nominee was to be chosen." The article notes that the author is assistant general counsel to Dow Jones & Co., publisher of the *Wall Street Journal.*

and the press. Subsequently, the President "could even interview candidates personally, rather than inviting a single choice, already selected by staff members, to a job-offer luncheon." The FBI reports on those not chosen, "could presumably be kept truly secret, because only senior Justice Department and White House officials would ever see them."[30]

While calling on the President to implement various reforms, the Senate Democratic Task Force on the Confirmation Process declined to recommend that he open up the process of selecting nominees. However, the Task Force drew attention to the fact that the President's selection process "is conducted, for the most part, in private"[31] — whereas in reviewing Presidential nominations, "the Senate has made the determination to conduct a significant aspect of its nomination process in public."[32]

If a formal measure were introduced in the Senate calling on the President to make his selection process more open,[33] at least two basic objections might be expected. First, opening up the selection process in response to Senate urging might be viewed as relinquishment by the President of a constitutional power of his office — namely, the power to select a nominee under whatever conditions that he prefers. Explicit concerns over the President's constitutional power to make Supreme Court nominees prompted President Bush to react warily (and Senate leaders of the President's party to react negatively) to formal calls that he receive Senate "advice" on Supreme Court nominees;[34] the same consideration might make a President object to formal calls from the Senate that he make more public the process by which he chooses a Supreme Court nomination.

Second, it might be argued that a more open selection process — particularly one in which the White House identified prospective nominees to the Court – would cause the process to became more politicized. The designation of official candidates under White House consideration arguably would generate intense political pressures – from Members of Congress, the public at large, interest groups, etc. – complete with ambitious lobbying and public relations efforts mounted on behalf of prospective nominees. From this perspective, opening up

---

[30] Tofel, Four Steps, p. 22.

[31] Task Force, Report, p. S896. "The President's selection process," the Task Force continued, "involves background investigations, including an investigation conducted by the Federal Bureau of Investigation. Access to this information is controlled by the President, and he selects which, if any, of his advisors may review that information. Only such information as the President chooses to divulge is released to the public." *Ibid.*

[32] *Ibid.*

[33] For example, by publicly identifying a list of potential nominees, prior to making his choice.

[34] See statements of President Bush, Senate Republican Leader Bob Dole of Kansas, and Senator Strom Thurmond of South Carolina (ranking Republican on the Judiciary Committee), which are quoted in a preceding subsection of this report under the heading "Senate's Advisory Role."

the selection process could be seen as increasing the influence of political considerations on a President's selection, while decreasing the weight that otherwise might be assigned to prospective nominees' legal qualifications.

Executive's Investigation of a Prospective Nominee

Another part of the selection process on need of improvement, according to some critics, is the executive branch's investigation of prospective Supreme Court nominees.

Criticism of executive investigative performance emerged particularly in connection with the Senate's consideration in October 1991 of Anita Hill's sexual harassment allegations against Supreme Court nominee Clarence Thomas. For example, one magazine column reported that Senators "say their staffs must run field investigations because they cannot trust the FBI to be thorough and responsive. Anita Hill's name, for example, never showed up in five FBI investigations of Thomas, despite rumors of her allegations."[35] Reflecting these concerns, a former general counsel to the House Judiciary Committee recommended that the FBI "conduct a much more thorough field investigation of prospective nominees before they are named by the president."[36] Subsequently, a member of the Judiciary Committee, Senater DeConcine, wrote that the Thomas nomination, as well as the earlier, abortive Supreme Court nomination of Douglas H. Ginsburg in 1987, "demonstrated the imperfections of the Executive Branch's capability to investigate and evaluate nominees prior to appointment."[37]

Following Senate confirmation of the Thomas nomination on October 15, 1991, the White House considered possible changes in the way the executive investigates the backgrounds of prospective nominees. One reform proposal under White House consideration, it was reported, would have created a new Justice

---

[35] Gergen, David. How to Improve the Process. *U.S. News $ World Report,* v. 111, October 28, 1991. p.39.

[36] Nellis, Joseph L. An Imperfect Proceeding. *National law Journal,* v. 14, October 28, 1991. p. 16. (Hereafter cited as Nellis, Imperfect Proceeding)

[37] DeConcini, Senator Dennis. Examining the Process, p. 14.
On October 29, 1987 President Ronald Reagan announced his intention to nominate Judge Ginsburg, of the U.S. Court of Appeals for the District of Columbia Circuit, to the Supreme Court. On November 7, 1987, however, at the request of Judge Ginsburg, President Reagan withdrew the nomination before it was received by the Senate. The withdrawal was precipitated by media reports and Judge Ginsburg's admission that as a young man he had smoked marijuana. This fact had not been uncovered in the FBI's earlier background investigation of the prospective nominee. See Cohodas, Nadine. Ginsburg Hurt Badly by Marijuana Admission. *Congressional Quarterly Weekly Report,* v. 45, November 7, 1987. pp. 2714-16; Mauro, Tony. How the Reporters Got the Dope. *Legal Times,* v. 10, November 16, 1987. p. 15.

Department arm to deal only with confirmations.[38] Nonetheless, on October 24, 1991, in a heavily publicized statement devoted to reform of the confirmation process,[39] President Bush made no references to the prenomination investigation phase.[40]

The report of the Senate Democratic Task Force on the Confirmation Process, however, did refer to the executive's investigative role. Released on February 4, 1992 by the Senate Majority Leader, the Task Force report declared:

> The most critical evaluation of potential nominees occurs before submission to the Senate. If the process functions properly, unsuitable candidates will be screened out by the President *before* they are nominated. The responsibility for screening nominees lies first and foremost with the President and his administration. Their investigation must be thorough and complete. It is not in the interest of any party for unfit candidates to be nominated, with the Senate left to identify and reject such an unfit nominee.[41] (Emphasis by Task Force)

In the Democratic Task Force's view, the executive branch does not go far enough in providing assurances about the backgrounds of the nominees it has investigated:

> Despite the utilization of extensive resources in the Government... to review the character, qualifications and fitness of a nominee, at present only one formal certification of nominees is prepared: that of the Office of Government Ethics. This certification is based solely on a review of the financial information submitted by a nominee pursuant to the Ethics in Government Act, and reports to the appropriate Senate committee [on] the nominee's compliance with applicable laws and regulations governing conflict of interests with respect to the nominee's proposed duties.[42]

---

[38] Devroy, Ann. Bush, Biden Discuss Confirmation Ills. *Washington Post,* October 22, 1991. p. A5.

[39] Bush, Remarks to Public Administration Groups (see footnote 15) pp. 1495-1500.

[40] The President, however, indicated the executive's willingness, once nominees were selected, to try to process background information about nominees more expeditiously. The President declared: "We will redouble our efforts to ensure that nominees complete all their required paperwork promptly, and will respond promptly to requests for further important information. I've asked our Office of the White House Counsel and Office of Government Ethics to see that our regulations and clearance procedures do not, however, discourage public service. I am committed to an ethical administration, but we must ensure that our rules have not become so detailed and so onerous as to scare good, honest people away from public service." *Ibid.*, p. 1497.

[41] Democratic Task Force, Report (see footnote 14), p. S.897.

[42] *Ibid.*

Besides providing the above-noted certification, the Task Force said, the executive branch should certify that its files "contain no adverse information on a nominee that is not explained or disclosed in the reports to the Senate."[43]

Another suggestion for improving the executive branch's investigation of Supreme Court nominees would be to allow more time for the investigation to be conducted. Presidents typically make their selection of a Supreme Court nominee within days of a retirement announcement by a vacating Justice. The quickness of the executive's investigation and selection process is in contrast to the months of deliberations which the Senate has devoted to each of President Bush's and Reagan's Supreme Court Nominations. "This allocation of time should be substantially reversed," one legal commentator has suggested.[44]

The failure of the FBI's initial background investigation of Judge Thomas to come upon Professor Hill's grievances also raised the question of whether the Senate should rely less on the executive and enhance its own investigative capabilities. Among those urging the Senate to expand its investigatory operations for future Supreme Court nominees was the Alliance of Justice, a national association of civil rights organizations which had opposed the Thomas nomination. The Alliance stated its position in this way:

> Because the FBI considers the White House, not the Senate, as its client, the Senate should create a permanent, professional, nonpartisan investigations office to examine the background of nominees. The Senate cannot afford to rely on an agency under the control of this President. In the past, when faced with an executive branch reluctant to provide data, Congress established such permanent, nonpartisan offices as the Congressional Budget Office and the Office of Technology Assessment.[45]

---

43 *Ibid.*, p. S898. "In the event," the Task Force added, "that the executive Branch investigations reveal adverse information which is viewed as not disqualifying, and the President nonetheless proceeds to nominate the candidate, the President's counsel should so inform a committee in a confidential communication or meeting." *Ibid.*

44 Tofel, Four Steps (see footnote 29), p. 26.

45 Alliance for Justice Judicial Selection Project. *Year End Report; December 1991.* Washington, Alliance for Justice, December 1991. pp. 12-13. (Hereafter cited as Alliance for Justice, *Year End Report*)
Quite similar to the Alliance's case is the following argument for establishing an Office of Nominations in the Senate: "...an Office of Nominations would put investigations of presidential nominees in the hands of experts whose only allegiance was to the institution of the Senate – not to the White House, or to any individual senator or group of senators. This could be of critical value as the Senate seeks to fulfill its advice-and-consent function under the Constitution. The FBI would still be available to supplement committee resources, where necessary." Wegman, Richard. The Case for an Office of Nominations. *Legal Times,* v. 14, November 11, 1991. p. 24. The article notes that the author was chief counsel and staff director

Senate Judiciary Committee Investigation of Nominees

A second general object of proposed reform has been the process by which the Senate Judiciary Committee investigates the qualifications of a Supreme Court nominee. Proposed reforms in this area would affect the purpose and nature of the pre-hearing investigation by Judiciary Committee staff, the notice given to the nominee of what to expect at the confirmation hearings, the access which Members and staff have to confidential information about the nominee, and the procedures for dealing with unauthorized "leaks" of such information.

Other proposed changes would end the longstanding practice of nominees appearing before the Judiciary Committee, or seek in other ways to deemphasize the importance of hearings in the confirmation process. Still other changes would clarify the extent to which nominees are responsible to respond to Committee questioning, place limits on the repetitiousness or length of committee questioning, establish more definite guidelines as to when hearings should be closed to the public, and provide for other special hearings procedures to follow when considering misconduct allegations against a nominee, including the option of using non-Senators to cross-examine hearing witnesses.

Focus and Nature of Committee Staff Investigation

Some critics of the confirmation process have urged that Judiciary Committee staff devote their pre-hearing investigative work exclusively to the nominee's *public and professional record.* Taking this approach, committee research and preparation would focus on the nominee's past writings, statements and actions in public life and in the legal profession — with the central objective being to learn as much as possible about the nominee's legal qualifications, political and social views, and judicial philosophy. Meanwhile, fact-finding into the *private affairs* of the nominee (including his or her financial holdings), and into questions of *possible nominee misconduct*, wold be left to others — FBI investigators, GAO auditors, or a new investigative entity that would be separate from the Judiciary Committee.

One proposal reflecting this view would establish in the Senate an Office of Nominations to conduct background investigations on Presidential nominations in general.[46]

---

for the Senate Governmental Affairs Committee from 1975 to 1981. (Hereafter cited as Wegman, Case for Office of Nominations)

[46] Wegman, Case for Office of Nominations, pp. 24, 41.

The arguments for such an office, according to its advocate, are that it would: put investigations in the hands of experts whose only allegiance is to the institution of the Senate — "not to the White House, nor to any individual senator or group of senators";[47] insure that sufficient time is allotted to do the job properly;[48] hold investigative data "more closely" than would the committees which eventually vote on the nominees;[49] enable presidential nominations "to be handled on a more consistent basis";[50] and allow Senators and committee staff more time *to concentrate on and prepare for policy issues* to be addressed at the confirmation hearings.[51] (Emphasis added)

Similar proposals have been made which would apply only to judicial nominations. Under one proposal, the Senate would "create a permanent, professional, nonpartisan investigations office to examine the background of nominees."[52] Under another proposed reform, applying only to Supreme Court nominations, the Senate would delegate its investigatory and fact-finding process not to a special investigative entity in the Senate but to a "blue ribbon commission composed of esteemed citizens devoted to the general welfare, rater than to party politics."[53]

While some have questioned whether committee staff should conduct investigations into the private lives of Supreme Court nominees, others have also raised questions about the proper extent of staff investigations into the nominees' public record. During Senate debate on the Clarence Thomas nomination, for instance, Senator John C. Danforth (R-MO) asserted that "to comb through prior speeches, taking what has been said in a political context as a foreshadowing of what might be said in a judicial context is mistaken, and as a foreshadowing of what might be said in a judicial context is mistaken, and it has the effect of

[47] *Ibid.*, p. 24.

[48] This, the author states, would be the case "assuming the Senate adopted a rule barring any committee from taking up a nomination until the Nomination Office had completed its work…." *Ibid.*

[49] The data would be more closely held, the author maintains, "because the fact-finding function would be carried out by individuals who were one step removed from those with a direct political stake in the nomination." *Ibid.*, p. 41.

[50] "This should be welcome news to the White House, and to nominees who are about to confront the process for the first time. Will the nominee's tax returns be examined? What degree of financial disclosure will be required? What ethical guidelines will apply? Currently each Senate panel adopts its own policy on these questions, and no attempt is made to apply a consistent approach by the standing committees." *Ibid.*

[51] *Ibid.*

[52] Alliance for Justice, *Year End Report,* p. 12. Such an office was needed, the report said, because "the FBI considers the White House, not the Senate, as its client" and because the Senate "cannot afford to rely on an agency under the control to this President."

[53] Forrester, Call for Integrity (see footnote 28), p. 19.

inviting Presidents of the United States, present and future, to send us nominations of total nonentities."[54] Senator Danforth referred disapprovingly to "all of the staff members who have been analyzing every footnote and every law review article" written by Judge Thomas.[55]

A contrasting perspective is that an exhaustive review of a nominee's public statements, even one taken primarily to find unfavorable information, may constitute "legitimate negative research."[56] Expressing this viewpoint at the end of the Thomas confirmation battle, one legal analyst praised researchers "who dared comb through Thomas's speech texts to document his inflammatory attacks on Supreme Court precedents" or who examined his public statements "for signs of hypocrisy."[57]

Committee Notice to Nominee of What to Expect

Under established practice, the Senate Judiciary Committee already provides two forms of notice to Supreme Court nominees about questions that are likely to be asked. Prior to the confirmation hearings, a nominee receives from the Committee a questionnaire requesting not only biographical and financial disclosure information, but also responses to questions concerning the nominee's views about the Constitution and the law. The latter kinds of questions typically are "tailored" to that particular nominee, in order to elicit information of special interest to the Committee members in the context of that nomination. These questions are not exhaustive, nor is it a certainty that they will be posed to the nominee in identical or similar form at the hearings. Nonetheless, they provide an advance, and formalized, indication to the nominee of issues that are of interest or concern to at least some Members on the Judiciary Committee.

A second customary opportunity for Senators to alert the nominee about questions to expect comes during the "courtesy calls" which a nominee traditionally pays to individual Senate offices prior to the confirmation hearings. Senators provide this notice explicitly when they tell the nominee outright what

---

[54] Danforth, John C. Supreme Court of the United States. Remarks in the Senate. *Congressional Record,* daily Edition, v. 137, October 3, 1991. p. S14290.

[55] *Ibid.,* p. S14289.

[56] Taylor, Stuart, Jr. Taking Issue: In Defense of Dirt Digging. *Legal Times,* v. 14, October 21, 1991. p. 23. The author is identified as a senior writer with *The American Lawyer* magazine. *Ibid.*

[57] *Ibid.* In the context of the present discussion, the following might be considered an uncontroversial view of the proper role for Senate investigative staff: "The probe should include investigation of the person's professional record and also the person's views on crucial issues. This, of course, should include a careful review of past writings and speeches." Chemerinsky, Erwin. October Tragedy. *Southern California Law Review,* v. 65, May 1992. p. 1515. Some, however, might question at what point a "careful" review becomes an "excessive" review.

they (or other Senators) are likely to ask at the hearings, or implicitly when, during the courtesy call, they indicate what questions or issues are important to them at that point in time.

Notwithstanding these established practices, one proposed reform would place greater emphasis on committee notice to a nominee as to what to expect at the confirmation hearings. In the view of one legal analyst, for instance, the staff of the Judiciary Committee not only could devote the pre-hearing phase to extensive review of the nominee's public record but "should prepare and submit to the nominee a thorough written questionnaire on *every issue* that could be brought up later in committee."[58] (Emphasis added)

Similarly, the Senate Democratic Task Force on the Confirmation Process has recommended that all Senate committees which consider Presidential nominations "make clear, in advance, which subjects and documents will be the basis for questioning a nominee; in return, the nominee should be familiar with these matters, and prepared to answer questions about them."[59]

A report of the New York City Bar Association has called for even more comprehensive committee notice to Supreme Court nominees. "The Judiciary Committee," the report said, "should provide the nominee with advance notice of the *questions each Senator intends to ask* at the confirmation hearings, thus enabling the nominee to become familiar with the pertinent subjects and thereby contribute to a more useful, productive and efficient dialogue."[60] (Emphasis added)

These recommendations have particular relevance in light of controversies that have arisen at recent Supreme Court confirmation hearings over questions posed to the nominees. Some critics have maintained that, rather than seeking to better understand a nominee's views, questions at times were aimed at trapping or "tripping up" the nominee, in order to hurt his or her chances for confirmation. Providing advance notice of anticipated areas of questioning arguably would reduce the element of surprise or entrapment as a factor at the hearings; it also would afford a nominee the opportunity to deliberate over and prepare thoughtful responses to the questions that are likely to be posed.

At the same time, giving formal notice of planned areas of questioning could conceivably aggravate what some already perceive to be a problem at Supreme Court confirmation hearings — namely, "staged" performances by nominees who have rehearsed well in advance of the hearings on anticipation of certain

[58] Nellis, imperfect Proceeding (see footnote 36), p. 16.

[59] Democratic Task force, Report (see footnote 14), p. S898.

[60] Association of the Bar of the City of New York. *Report of the Ad Hoc Committee on the Senate Confirmation Process,* June 8, 1992. p. 4. (Hereafter cited as NYC Bar Association, Report)

questions. A related concern is that testimony by a nominee having the benefit of extensive preparation, and even "coaching" from the Administration, is less genuine (and less revealing of the nominee's intellectual ability and temperament) than testimony a nominee would supply on shorter, and less complete, notice. To elicit a less rehearsed view of the nominee, some have suggested that hearings be scheduled quickly — even within days after a nomination is announced.[61] This scenario would not necessarily preclude giving a nominee notice of what areas of questioning to expect, but, given time restrictions, it might limit how detailed the Judiciary Committee could be in mapping out those areas for the nominee's benefit.

Access to Confidential Information

Member and staff access to confidential information which the Senate Judiciary Committee receives about Supreme Court nominees has also been a focus of reform proposals. The adequacy of the Committee's confidentiality procedures emerged as an issue on October 6, 1991. That day the newspaper *Newsday* and National Public Radio disclosed allegations of sexual harassment by law professor Anita Hill against Supreme Court nominee Clarence Thomas, allegations which earlier had been filed with the Judiciary Committee on a confidential basis. Amid concerns that information maintained by the Judiciary Committee pertaining to the Hill allegations might have been "leaked" to the press, the Senate on October 24, 1991 (nine days after it had confirmed Judge Thomas) approved S. Res 202. The resolution provided for appointment of a special counsel to conduct an investigation into, among other things, whether there had been any unauthorized disclosure from within the Committee of "nonpublic confidential information" pertaining to the Thomas nomination.[62]

---

[61] See Ceol, Dawn. Experts Disagree on Confirmation Hearings. *Washington Times,* September 24, 1991. p. A3. The article reports, among other things, the suggestion of Senator Patrick Leahy (D-VT), a member of the Judiciary Committee, that Supreme Court nominees appear before the Judiciary Committee within 48 hours of their nomination so that, in the words of the *Times'* reporter, "the White House would have no time for coaching." See also Tofel, Four Steps (see footnote 29), p. 26, in which author urges that Supreme Court confirmation hearings commence within *one week* of the date of the nomination.

[62] Resolution Relative to the Appointment of Special Counsel – Senate Resolution 202. *Congressional Record,* Daily Edition, v. 137, October 24, 1991. pp. S15122-34, with full text of the resolution on pp. S15133-34. The resolution provided that the special counsel also investigate "matters related to [savings and loan executive] Charles Keating by the Select Committee on Ethics."

Further, S. Res. 202 provided that upon receipt of an investigatory report from the special counsel the Senate Majority Leader and the Minority Leader (or their designees) would not only determine whether any disciplinary action should be taken against any Senator or Senate

The controversy over news media disclosure of the Anita Hill allegations was complicated by uncertainty in the Senate as to the kind of documents which might actually have been made available to the press. Professor Hill's allegations of sexual harassment were initially contained both in an FBI report on file with the Committee and in telefaxed statements which she supplied directly to the Committee. The possibility that an FBI-supplied background report or a Committee-obtained statement might have been supplied to the press prompted different kinds of reform initiatives. One, aimed at putting greater restrictions on *FBI reports*, came from President Bush in October 1991. Another initiative, aimed at making *Committee-obtained or Committee-generated information* about nominees more accessible to Senators not serving on the Judiciary Committee, came in June 1992 from Senator Biden, the Committee's Chairman.

Access to FBI Reports

Soon after the October 15, 1991 confirmation of Judge Thomas to the Supreme Court, Senate access to confidential FBI background information about Presidential nominees became a point of contention between the White House and the Judiciary Committee. The dispute arose when President Bush ordered new restrictions imposed on the access of Senate committees to FBI reports on nominees. While this action produced sharp initial conflict between the White House and the Judiciary Committee, the two sides eventually reached an agreement on certain clarifications to the rules which govern this part of the judicial confirmation process.

The President's new restrictions were announced on October 24.[63] Under the restrictions, only Judiciary Committee *Members* would be allowed to see FBI reports on a Supreme Court nominee; such access would no longer be given to investigative staff who previously had been designated by the Committee Chairman or the Ranking Minority Member to see FBI background reports.[64]

---

employee ("who may have violated any rule of the Senate or any Senate committee"); under the resolution, they also were to make "recommendations for any changes *in Federal law or in Senate rules* that should be made to prevent similar unauthorized disclosures in the future." *Ibid., p.* S15134. (Emphasis added)

[63] There were two announcements of the restrictions – one a speech by President Bush devoted to the topics of public service and public faith in government service, the other a White House "Fact Sheet" detailing specific reform proposals by the President "to enhance the public's confidence in the appointment and confirmation process." See U.S. President, 1989-93 (Bush). Remarks to Representatives of Public Administration Groups on Public Service, October 24, 1991. *Weekly Compilation of Presidential Documents,* v. 27, October 28, 1991. pp. 1495-500 (hereafter cited as Bush, Remarks to Public Administration Groups); White House Office of the Press Secretary. *Fact Sheet,* October 24, 1991. 3 p. (Hereafter cited as White House, Fact Sheet)

[64] Bush, Remarks to Public Administration Groups, pp. 1497-98; White House, *Fact Sheet*, p. 1.

Further, the examined material thenceforth would consist only of summaries of FBI reports, rather than full accounts, and Committees would "not be permitted to keep copies of summaries."[65] This action, the President explained, "preserves confidentiality. In my view, it protects nominees. It protects potential witnesses against the nominees. And it protects the members of Congress."[66]

The Judiciary Committee, However, took issue with the President. On November 21, 1991 the Committee unanimously passed a resolution calling on President Bush to restore the previous agreement that existed between the Committee and the Administration. Under that agreement, the resolution noted, Committee Members and FBI-cleared investigative staff on the Committee had enjoyed access to FBI background checks on judicial nominees and on nominees to U.S. Attorney and U.S. Marshal positions. Without a restoration of the agreement, the resolution warned, "Committee consideration of nominees will be slowed, and will require more extensive investigation."[67] This continued to be the bi-partisan position of the Committee into January 1992, at which point Judiciary Committee members were predicting "massive delays in filling judicial vacancies" if no resolution were reached.[68]

A similar admonition to the President came from the Senate Democratic Task Force on the Confirmation Process in a report released on February 4, 1992. The Task Force, discussing not only nominations referred to the Judiciary Committee, but those referred to other committees as well, warned:

> If the Administration restricts the background information on nominees it provides to Senate committees so that the committees cannot adequately evaluate the qualifications and fitness of nominees, it will be necessary for the Senate to expand its capabilities for Senate committees to conduct thorough investigations of nominees.[69]

---

[65] White House, *Fact Sheet*, p. 1.

[66] Bush, Remarks to Public Administration Groups, p. 1498.

[67] Committee Resolution Draft 2, adopted by Senate Committee on the Judiciary, November 21, 1991. See also Simpson, Glenn R. Judiciary Tells Bush: End Restrictions on FBI Data. *Roll Call*, v. 37, November 25, 1992. pp. 1, 21. (Hereafter cited as Simpson, Judiciary Tells Bush)

[68] Klaidman, Daniel. Nominations Impasse May Be Ending, *Legal Times*, v. 14, January 20, 1992. p. 6.

[69] Democratic Task Force, Report (see footnote 14), p. S898. The Task Force described what might be entailed if the Senate expanded its investigative capabilities: "Committees with investigators now on staff might expand their existing personnel; special investigative counsel could be retained on an as-needed basis; such counsel could be retained on a full-time basis by a centralized unit in the Senate and detailed to different committees as required; or investigators and auditors could be detailed from existing Federal agencies, such as the General Accounting Office." *Ibid.*

Soon thereafter, on February 7, 1992, the White House and Senate Judiciary Committee settled their differences over the Committee's access to FBI reports on nominees. A new memorandum of understanding (signed by the Counsel to the President, the Chairman of the Senate Judiciary Committee, and the Ranking Minority Member on the Committee) largely reinstated the 1989 White House-Judiciary Committee agreement that President Bush in effect had nullified in October 1991. Under the new understanding, full FBI reports on judicial nominees would again be provided to the Committee and access to FBI reports would again be allowed to designated staff as well as to Senators on the Committee.[70]

In a concession to the President, however, the new memo added these clarifications: 1) Document control experts from Senate security will periodically review the effectiveness of procedures used by the Judiciary Committee to maintain physical custody of files; b) photocopying or verbatim reproduction of FBI reports is prohibited; c) notes and memoranda which are "derived from FBI reports" will be secured in a manner identical to FBI reports and, at the conclusion of Senate action, will either be destroyed or kept secure.[71]

A significant postscript to this controversy occurred on May 5, 1992, when the report of the Special Counsel investigating the Hill/Thomas "leaks" was released pursuant to S. Res. 202.[72] The report said that the results of its investigation had established that neither a "hard copy" of the FBI report on Professor Hill's allegations, nor the contents of the FBI report, were "disseminated outside the Senate in whole or in part, contrary to the impression created" by the broadcast and print news media stories on the allegations. By contrast, it found that an "unauthorized disclosure" of written allegations by Professor Hill made to the Judiciary Committee had "played a significant role in the publication" of the Hill allegations on National Public Radio. The report added, however, that its investigation had been "unable to identify the Senate source of the document delivered" to NPR.[73]

---

[70] Memorandum of Understanding between Senate Judiciary Committee and White House Counsel, February 7, 1992. 3 p.

[71] *Ibid.*, p. 2. Rather than signifying a new procedure, however, the memorandum's ban on photocopying and note-taking apparently only formalized well-established practice. Senator Biden noted that prior to the White House's imposition of restrictions on Judiciary Committee access to FBI reports on nominees, Committee Members had been allowed only to read the reports and could not copy them or keep notes. Simpson, Judiciary Tells Bush, p. 21.

[72] U.S. Senate. *Report of Temporary Special Independent Counsel Pursuant to Senate resolution 202.* Senate Document No. 102-20, Part 1, 102d Cong., 2d Sess. Washington, U.S. Govt. Print. Off., 1992. 80 p.

[73] *Ibid.*, pp. 2-3.

Access to Committee Information

Although concluding that Committee-obtained information had played a part in news media reporting of the Hill allegations, the Special Counsel 's report declined to recommend any changes in the Judiciary Committee's rules governing access to confidential information. The report observed that:

> ...the Judiciary Committee has no formal rules which address the handling of confidential information or investigative materials. Nonetheless, the Committee does have well-established guidelines and practices regarding the treatment of FBI reports and investigative materials. That these customs and practices are *widely Known and adhered to* is evidenced by the fact that, without exception, every senator and staff person we interviewed characterized the statement of Anita Hill and the supplemental FBI report as "confidential" documents whose disclosure would be improper.[74] (Emphasis added)

The Special Counsel's report added that it could "find no basis for criticizing the procedures of the Judiciary Committee or otherwise attributing the Hill disclosures to any shortcomings in [the Committee's] internal practices." Nonetheless, the report said, "it may be worthwhile for all committees to review their existing procedures in handling confidential material and to consider the utility of written guidelines."[75]

Subsequently, in a June 25, 1992 Senate floor speech, Chairman Biden addressed the manner in which the Committee handles investigative information. Senator Biden remarked that no aspect of the Supreme Court confirmation process had been "more widely discussed than our handling of Professor Hill's allegations against Judge Thomas before those charges became public." Stating his belief that the Committee investigated the Hill charges properly, Senator Biden added, nonetheless, that he also believed "there are some things we should do differently in the future for the purposes of improving public confidence in our handling of investigative matters."[76] He announced that henceforth the following three changes would apply to information that the Judiciary Committee obtains about a Supreme Court nominee on a confidential basis:

- all sources "will be notified that any information obtained by the committee will be placed in the FBI file on the nominee, and shared on

---

[74] *Ibid.*, p. 71.
[75] *Ibid.*, p. 73.
[76] Biden, Reform of Confirmation Process (see footnote 18), p. S8866.

that confidential basis" with all 100 Senators before the Senate votes on the nomination;

- All Senators will be invited to attend closed briefing sessions about the nominee and, "under rigorous restrictions to protect confidentiality," to inspect all documents and reports compiled by the Committee on the nominee; and,
- the Committee will "routinely conduct a closed session with each nominee — face to face, on the record, under oath — about all investigative charges against that person," with the transcripts of the session available to all Senators.[77]

Senator Biden explained that he did not want the Judiciary Committee "ever again to be place in the awkward position of possessing information about a Supreme Court nominee which it has pledged to keep confidential from other Members of the Senate, as we did with Professor Hill's charges." Further, he wished to "ensure that *all* Senators are aware of *any* charges in our possession." (Emphases added) A closed session with each nominee on a routine basis, he said, was called for because "ultimately, the question with respect to investigations of a Supreme Court nominee is the credibility and character of that nominee… . "The three steps he outlined, Senator Biden concluded, "will increase confidence in the Committee's investigative procedures and the seriousness with which we take such matters as part of the confirmation process."[78]

A more critical view of Senator Biden's reform measures was expressed by the *Washington Times*. In an editorial, the *Times* questioned the wisdom of making investigative data about Supreme Court nominees available to all Senators. Under the changes announced by its Chairman, The *Times* said, said, the Judiciary Committee "is no longer to be entrusted with the sole responsibility [of] weighing the dozens of charges — many of them unsubstantiated and anonymous — that typically flow in at nomination time." Instead, the editorial maintained, "charges will now be aired to the entire Senate, giving accusers a much wider and potentially more receptive audience and increasing exponentially the chance that the charges will not remain confidential."[79]

---

[77] *Ibid.*

[78] *Ibid.*

[79] Sen. Biden's New Rules. *Washington Times*, July 8, 1992. p. G2. The editorial also criticized the holding of routine closed sessions on investigative charges against the nominee: "…these inquisitions will be closed, out of the public eye, with copies of transcripts of the proceedings floating throughout the Senate corridors. This can only make the job of the hatchet-wielding leakers and reporters that much easier." *Ibid.*

Dealing with 'Leaks'

Proposals to reform the confirmation process have also included calls that procedures be put in place on the Senate to insure that a prompt investigation is conducted and appropriate punitive action is taken in the event of any future "leak" of confidential information regarding a nominee.

These calls were spurred by the controversy surrounding the unauthorized release to the press of confidential allegations against Supreme Court nominee Clarence Thomas. While the Senate's immediate concern (following its October 15, 1991 vote confirming Judge Thomas) was to appoint a special counsel to determine who released the confidential Thomas information, concerns also were expressed about the Senate's responsibilities in general regarding "leaks" of confidential information. Punitive legislation designed to prevent future leaks was first introduced on October 17, 1991 by Senator Mitch McConnell (R-KY). Under S. 1839, Senator McConnell explained, any "unauthorized or unlawful disclosure of any FBI background investigation report to any unauthorized party" could result in criminal penalties, including a prison term and a fine. The bill, Senator McConnell added, would apply the same criminal penalties "to anyone who knowingly solicits or receives such information."[80]

On October 24, 1991, as the Senate deliberated on, and then approved, a resolution appointing a special counsel to investigate unauthorized disclosures related to the Thomas nomination,[81] Senate Majority Leader George Mitchell (D-ME) declared it would be wrong for the Senate to take the position that "only one leak matters":

> I submit to my colleagues that is the wrong measure to be sending to the Senate. Every leak is wrong. Every leak is bad. Every leak should be condemned. Every leak should be deplored. Every leak should be investigated and persons punished. And that is what I have sought to do from the beginning.[82]

---

[80] McConnell, Mitch. Preventing the Disclosure of Confidential Information on the Senate Advice and Consent Process. Remarks in the Senate. *Congressional Record,* Daily Edition, v. 137, October 17, 1991. p. S14917-18.

[81] Resolution Relative to the Appointment of Special Counsel – Senate Resolution 202. *Congressional Record,* Daily Edition, v. 137, October 24, 1991. pp. S15122-34.
The resolution adopted by the Senate, S. Res. 202, also mandated that the special counsel investigate disclosures of non-public confidential information from senate documents in connection with the investigation of matters related to Charles Keating by the Select Committee on Ethics. See *Ibid.,* p. S15133, for text of resolution.

[82] *Ibid.,* p. S15129.

That same day, October 24, President Bush expressed similar sentiments about unauthorized disclosures of confidential nominee information. Congress, he declared "should establish a mechanism for investigating congressional leaks thoroughly, professionally, promptly." He added that he had just met with Senate leaders "from both parties, and they agree that we must prevent future leaks and establish a suitable mechanism for investigating them swiftly, bringing culprits to justice."[83]

Subsequently, the Senate Democratic Task Force on the Confirmation Process urged each Senate committee which processes nominations to adopt a rule on improper disclosure of confidential information. "Any unauthorized release of confidential information in the confirmation process," the Task Force declared in a report released on February 4, 1992, "should be promptly investigated and fully punished." Under the Task Force's recommendations, if a committee does not promptly undertake an investigation of a suspected leak, "the Senate Leadership should be authorized to direct the Senate Legal Counsel to appoint an outside counsel to conduct an Investigation."[84] Any unauthorized release, the Task Force said, "should be swiftly and severely punished" — with staff subject to the possible sanction of termination of employment, and a Senator "subject to consideration by the Select Committee on Ethics."[85]

Whether Nominee's Presence is Desirable

Some observers have questioned the desirability of having Supreme Court nominees appear personally before the Judiciary Committee. It is generally agreed that this practice constituted an important benefit to the Senate, as it affords

[83] Bush, Remarks to Public Administration Groups (see footnote 63), p. 1498. The President's use of the phrase "congressional leaks" addressed the problem of unauthorized *Senate* disclosures, without identifying the *executive branch* as another possible source of future leaks. Coincidentally, on the same day that the President made these remarks, Majority Leader Mitchell expressed concerns about a press report that "allies" of the White House, "to inoculate" a nominee against possible attack, leaked his admission that he had used marijuana and cocaine (words quoted from April 6, 1990 newsletter *Congressional Insight,* part of which was inserted by Senator Mitchell into the Congressional Record). Senator Mitchell declared: "It would be a massive injustice – a massive injustice-for the Senate to be blamed for a leak that was carried out by the White House handlers of a nominee to gain a tactical and political advantage, if in fact that occurred. And I emphasize I do not know if that occurred." Mitchell, George J. In: Resolution Relative to the Appointment of Special Counsel – Senate Resolution 202. *Congressional Record,* Daily Edition, v. 137, October 24, 1991. p. S15129.

[84] Democratic Task Force, Report, p. S898 (see footnote 14). "Within ten days of any report revealing an unauthorized disclosure by a Senate employee, his or her employer should report to the Senate Leadership the disciplinary action taken." *Ibid.*

[85] *Ibid.*

Members the opportunity to pose questions directly to the nominee and to assess the nominee's intellect and temperament based on his or her performance under pressure. On the other hand, some observers have suggested that a nominee's presence may also have undesirable effects — for example, creating a sense of confrontation between the nominee and Committee members, exposing a nominee to hurtful charges in full view of millions of Americans, or eliciting from the nominee testimony which is calculated to please Committee members while concealing the nominee's actual views.

Reflecting such concerns, a non-governmental task force of lawyers in the wake of the 1987 controversy over the nomination of Robert H. Bork recommended that nominees for the Court no longer testify before the committee. The Task Force on Judicial Selection, established by the Twentieth Century Fund, contended that the Supreme Court confirmation process had "become very much a national referendum on the appointment, with media campaigns, polling techniques, and political rhetoric that distract attention from, and sometimes completely distort, the legal qualifications of the nominee."[86]

This recommendation, however, received little support at the time it was issued, even from Judiciary Committee members who had supported Judge Bork. Among those disagreeing with the report was Senator Strom Thurmond, the Committee's Ranking Minority Member and former Chairman, who said: "If the Senate is responsible for confirming Supreme Court nominees we ought to have a right to cross examine individuals. Or otherwise, how would you get difficult questions answered?"[87] Another Committee member who had supported the Bork nomination, Senator Orrin G. Hatch (R-UT) said the task force recommendation was "a nice idea in theory, but practically it won't work."[88]

Questions about the desirability of Supreme Court nominees testifying arose again in September 1991, after the first round of confirmation hearings for nominee Clarence Thomas. Critics, including some Judiciary Committee members, expressed concern about Judge Thomas's sincerity in his testimony when he tempered, or divorced himself from, controversial positions he had taken in earlier speeches and writings. "Observers," one news account reported, "were reminded of the incentives for candidates to check their opinions at the hearing

---

[86] The 10-member Task Force was headed by Hught Carey, former Governor of New York (and, prior to that, former Member of the U.S. House of Representatives). Its analysis and recommendations were published in book form; see *Judicial Roulette*: *Report of the Twentieth Century Fund Task Force on Judicial Selection*. New York, Priority Press Publications, 1988. 145 p.

[87] Cirton, Zachary. Should Court Nominees Be Left Off Hook? *Roll Call*, v. 33, May 8, 1988. p. 15.

[88] *Ibid.*

room door."[89] One of these observers, law professor Walter Dellinger of Duke University Law School, argued that confirmation hearings were "distorting the process and playing too central a role in evaluating the nominee." A solution he said, would be for a nominee not to testify, and for Senators to rely solely on the nominee's past record in evaluating his or her fitness.[90] Similar sentiments were expressed in November 1991 at an American Bar Association "roundtable" on the Supreme Court confirmation process.[91]

The Senate Democratic Task Force on the Confirmation Process, however, disagreed with these recommendations. It urged instead that committees "continue to invite nominees to appear at confirmation hearings."[92] Confirmation hearings, the Task Force maintained, should consist of a "productive *exchange* of view." (Emphasis added) Furthermore, the Task Force asserted:

> The American people have a right to hear the testimony of nominees, wherein they describe their competence and their positions on issues of public policy relating to the office for which they have been nominated. The public hearing is an integral part of the confirmation process for determining the fitness of a nominee to fill a specific position; it is important for the nominee to actively participate in the process. As the only public aspect of the appointment process, the Senate hearing is necessary so that the public may witness and judge a nominee's fitness and qualifications."[93]

Upon release of the Task Force report, Majority Leader Mitchell stated that he, too, favored the continued appearance of nominees at confirmation hearings. In a February 4, 1992 floor statement, Senator Mitchell rejected the notion that confirmation hearings are unfair to nominees:

---

[89] Biskupic, Thomas Hearings Illustrate Politics (see Footnote 21), p. 2689.

[90] *Ibid.*

[91] At the "roundtable," one of the four panelists, University of Chicago law professor Michael W. McConnell, contended that the appearance of the nominee before the Judiciary Committee, "if he appears at all, ought to be a relatively minor footnote. Otherwise, the principal attribute being judged is television style rather than a whole career." Although not explicitly opposing nominee appearances at confirmation hearings, another panelist, Judge Alex Kozinski, of the U.S. Court of Appeals for the Ninth Circuit, remarked, "I like the suggestion of de-emphasizing the hearings and re-emphasizing the public record." Goldberg, Stephanie B., ed. What's the Alternative? A Roundtable on the Confirmation Process. *American Bar Association Journal,* v. 78, January 1992. pp. 41 (McConnell) and 45 (Kozinski). (Hereafter cited as Goldberg, What's the Alternative?)

[92] Democratic Task Force, Report (see footnote 14), p. S898.

[93] *Ibid.,* p. 896. See also Ford, Wendell H. Remarks in the Senate. *Congressional Record,* Daily Edition, v. 138, February 4, 1992. p. S899.

> ...it is hard to imagine anything more unfair than a return to the earlier era in which the Senate voted on nominees without giving them the opportunity to present their views to the public. The President knows this, and so do nominees — they come to testify if their own free will. Indeed, it has been my observation that nominees whose confirmations are contested are among those most eager to come to make their case.
>
> Like many other criticisms of the confirmation process, the complaint that nominees are obliged to appear before our committees is unfounded. And for all the concern expressed over such hearings, they create an atmosphere that is fairer to all involved, and more likely to result in the confirmation of a worthy nominee, than does the alternative.[94]

Whether to Deemphasize the Confirmation Hearings

Another proposed approach to reform of the Supreme Court confirmation process would be to deemphasize the role played by hearings. Among options available on such approach might be the following: The hearings could be held soon after the Senate received the nomination (thereby precluding an extended pre-hearing period during which committee and news media attention are focused almost exclusively on the upcoming hearings); the number of days of hearings and the number of witnesses permitted to testify could both be reduced; all or part of the hearings could be closed to the pubic, or at least closed to the electronic media; or the hearings could focus primarily or exclusively on the public record of the nominee, deemphasizing or eliminating the nominee's personal appearance as an ingredient in the hearings.

Various legal scholars have urged that the Senate deemphasize the confirmation hearings in the Supreme Court nomination process. Illustrative of this viewpoint, two law professors recently elaborated on why, in their view, it is "in the Senate's own interest to place less weight: in the confirmation hearings:

> Of particular importance is the threat to judicial independence posed by ongoing conversations between the Department of Justice and the White House on the one hand, and the nominee on the other. These conversations frequently involve matters likely to reach the Court. It is unfortunate if the nominee has been schooled in the views of the current Administration. Moreover, the hearings sometimes become mired in irrelevant or misleading factors, such as the nominee's telegenic qualities and how the various

---

[94] Mitchell, George. Remarks in the Senate. Visit to the Senate by Members of the British House of Commons. *Congressional Record*, v. 138, Daily Edition, February 4, 1992, p. S894. "As an aside," Senator Mitchell noted that "in the case of Supreme Court nominees, the Senate's rate of confirming justices has been higher since the advent of hearings than it was in the period before such hearings were conducted." *Ibid.*

> Senators 'look.' Televised competition between Senators and the nominee, or among the Senators, is hardly in the national interest. Finally, because of their immediacy and drama, the hearings tend to assume disproportionate importance. They can dwarf the much more relevant information provided by the pre-nomination record. The pre-nomination record is a far more reliable indicator of the nominee's views. The Senate should rely principally on that record, rather than a nominee's testimony, in deciding whether to consent to the nomination. Such an emphasis would reduce many of the problems of the current system.[95]

A quite different perspective on this issue, however, is provided by the Senate Democratic Task Force on the Confirmation Process. In its recently issued report, the Task Force did not directly address whether there should be less emphasis on confirmation hearings but seemed to suggest otherwise, by attaching unique importance to the role played by these hearings in the Senate's review of nominations:

> The Constitution assigns to the Senate alone the responsibility for reviewing Presidential nominations. In conducting this responsibility, the Senate has made the determination to conduct a significant aspect of its nomination process in public. *The confirmation hearing is the only point in the appointment process of Federal officials that offers the public an opportunity to evaluate the qualifications of a nominee.* The Senate has taken this obligation seriously and believes that the public hearing process is vital to the Senate's constitutional role of "advice and consent.'"[96] (Emphasis supplied by the Task Force)

---

[95] Strauss, David A., and Cass R. Sunstein. The Senate, the Constitution, and the Confirmation Process. *Yale Law Journal,* v. 101, May 1992. p. 1518. (Hereafter cited as Strauss and Sunstein, Senate and Constitution) In an introductory note Strauss is identified as a Professor of Law at University of Chicago Law School and as having "served as Special Counsel to the United States Senate Committee on the Judiciary in connection with the nomination of Justice David H. Souter to the Supreme Court." Sunstein is identified as Karl N. Llewellyn Professor of Jurisprudence, University of Chicago, Law School and Department of Political Science. *Ibid.,* p. 1491.

Likewise, Duke University law professor Walter Dellinger has expressed his belief that "the hearing has come to play a far too prominent role in the process." He notes that the Senate "went for 150 years without having nominees even appear" before the Senate Judiciary Committee. Goldberg; What's the Alternative?, pp. 41-42. In the same article, on p. 45, see also the comments of Judge Alex Kozinski of the U.S. Court of Appeals for the Ninth Circuit, in which he suggests that increased emphasis on the public record and deemphasis of hearings might discourage Presidents from nominating nominees who have no public record.

[96]. Democratic Task Force, Report (see Footnote 14), p. S896.

For their part, various legal scholars who have expressed concern about the emphasis placed on the confirmation hearings have noted the importance of hearings in making the Supreme Court confirmation process accessible to the people. "After the passage of the 17th Amendment

Subsequently, however, a cautionary note against attaching too much importance to confirmation hearings was sounded by one of the Task Force's five members, Senator Joseph R. Biden, Jr. In a June 25, 1992 floor speech, Senator Biden stressed that, in his view, confirmation hearings, "no matter how long, how fruitful, how thorough, cannot alone provide a sufficient basis for determining if a nominee merits a seat on our Supreme Court." Senator Biden said that Senators and the public, as "they did before there were confirmation hearings," should base their determination about a nominee on his or her record of service, writings, and speeches, on background investigative information, on a review of he nominee's experience in credentials, and on a "weighing of the views of the nominee's peers and colleagues." The role of the hearing process, Senator Biden maintained, had unfortunately been confused by "the burden of the trial analogy." That analogy, he asserted, was not valid:

> We have hearings not to prove a case against a nominee but, rather, in an effort to be fair to the nominee, and to give that nominee the chance to explain his or her record and writings before the Committee. Thus, the hearings can be the crowning jewel of the evaluation process, a final chance to clear up confusion, or firm up soft conclusions, but they cannot be the entire process itself as they have come to be viewed.
>
> Anything we can do to broaden the base upon which Senators make their decisions will be a valuable improvement on the confirmation process.[97]

Complicating any effort to deemphasize future confirmation hearings would be the presence of the news media. In the case of recent Supreme Court nominations which were Controversial, the hearings of the Senate Judiciary Committee were for the media important news events which accordingly received either complete or extensive live coverage of various television networks. Should the Senate wish to continue to formally interrogate Supreme Court nominees in public sessions, such a process will, in all likelihood, continue to occur in the

---

providing for the [popular] election of senators," one scholar writes, "it is very difficult to argue that one of the Senate's most important functions should not be made on the basis of very public record." Duke University law professor Walter Dellinger, in Goldberg, What's the Alternative?, p. 43.

See also Strauss and Sunstein, Senate and Constitution, pp. 1518-19, in which they write: "At least in their ideal form, [hearings] have an important educative function. Confirmation hearings might help inform the public of the actual and potential role of the Supreme Court, allowing diverse views to be expressed on that subject." They add, however, that "the current system offers only minor advances in public education, and it does so while introducing a range of distortions into the process."

[97] Biden, Reform of Confirmation Process (see footnote 18), S8865.

form of Judiciary Committee confirmation hearings.[98] To attempt to "deemphasize" such public events in a way that will significantly reduce intensive news media coverage might be difficult under any circumstances, and it may be impossible to do so when a nomination is controversial.

Responsibility of Nominee to Respond to Committee Questioning

Another issue at recent Supreme Court confirmation hearings has been the question of when it is appropriate for a nominee to decline to answer questions that are posed by members of the Judiciary Committee. Related to this has been the issue of what, if anything, Senators should do when a nominee declines to respond to questions that they believe should be answered.

Occasionally, questions posed at confirmation hearings have been criticized for calling on nominees to express positions on issues that might later come before the Supreme Court.[99] A nominee who expresses views in response to such questions, these critics maintain, could be viewed as prejudging the issue, compromising his or her impartiality to consider the issue in the future as a Justice on the Court. Further, it is argued, such questions undermine judicial independence, and put the confirmation process in an unfavorable light, by tempting nominees to make commitments on issues likely to come before the Court in order to persuade Senators to vote for their confirmation.[100]

---

[98] At least one legal scholar, however, has proposed that the Senate delegate its investigatory, fact-finding and hearing functions regarding Supreme Court nominations to a "a blue ribbon commission composed of esteemed citizens devoted to the general welfare." Forrester, Call for Integrity (see footnote 28), p. 19.

[99] For an examination of the periodic controversies that have arisen over the extent to which the Senate Judiciary Committee "properly may inquire into the judicial, political and social philosophies of a nominee," see Ross, William G. The Questioning of a Supreme Court Nominee at Senate Confirmation Hearings: Proposals for Accommodating the Needs of the Senate and Ameliorating the Fears of the Nominees. *Tulane Law Review,* v. 62, November 1987. pp. 109-74. (Hereafter cited as Ross, Questioning of Supreme Court Nominees)
See also U.S. Library of Congress. Congressional Research Service. *Questioning Supreme Court Nominees – A Recurring Issue.* Report No. 90-429 GOV, by Denis Steven Rutkus. Washington, September 6, 1990. p. 2 (discussing instances during 1959 and 1987 confirmation hearings of Supreme Court nominees Potter Stewart and Robert H. Bork, respectively, when members of the Senate Judiciary Committee debated among themselves what kinds of questions are appropriate to pose to a Supreme Court nominee).

[100] For instance, during Senate floor debate on the Supreme Court nomination of Clarence Thomas, Senator Strom Thurmond, the Ranking Minority Member on the Senate Judiciary Committee, remarked: "I believe it is inappropriate now for a nominee to the Supreme Court to answer specific questions about unsettled cases or issues that may come before the court. Each case must be decided upon the facts and questions of the law raised by that case after a judge has had time to fully contemplate a just decision. The impartiality and independence of the court would be compromised if a nominee had to prejudge any issue that may come before him." Thurmond,

For their part, Supreme Court nominees in some instances have been criticized for refusing to answer questions posed to them at their confirmation hearings. Sometimes they have been faulted for refusing to evaluate past Supreme Court rulings, for declining to discus even very basic questions of constitutional law, or for being unduly evasive when discussing them. [101] Responses to such questions, it has been argued, may be indispensable to the Senate in determining the nominee's views of the Constitution and the role which the Court should play in the American legal system — a determination which in turn may be essential for the Senate in assessing the fitness of the nominee to sit on the Court.[102]

The issue of when a Supreme Court nominee may properly decline to respond to Judiciary Committee questioning was of recurring interest to the Senate during the Presidencies of Ronald Reagan and George Bush. In 1986, two nominees, William H. Rehnquist and Antonin Scalia, declined to respond to various questions posed to them at their confirmation hearings. After favorably reporting the two nominations to the Senate, some members of the Judiciary Committee were reported to be "frustrated by their inability to extract information from the two men about their views of basic constitutional issues."[103]

The confirmation hearings in 1987 for Robert H. Bork and Anthony M. Kennedy proceeded differently. At the Bork hearings, according to one scholar, the members of the Judiciary Committee "probed with unprecedented

---

Strom. Nomination of Clarence Thomas, of Georgia, to be an Associate Justice of the Supreme Court of the United States. Remarks in the Senate. *Congressional Record,* Daily Edition, v. 137, October 4, 1991. p. S14386.

See also Silberman, Laurence. Attacking Activism, Judge Names Names. *Legal Times,* v. 15, June 22, 1992. p. 24; Berke, Richard. Senators Divided on Asking Souter His Abortion View. *New York Times,* July 25, 1990. pp. A1, A12.

[101] See Ross, Questioning of Supreme Court Nominees, pp. 125-39; Kurtz, Howard. Judicial Reticence Frustrates Senators. *Washington Post,* September 9, 1986. p. A4.

[102] In this vein, Senator Biden, Chairman of the Senate Judiciary Committee, remarked to nominee David H. Souter, at his confirmation hearings in September 1990, that "the past responsibilities you have had have not required you to enunciate your views in any detail on major constitutional issues and questions. As a result, we need your help for us to be able to understand your constitutional philosophy, the philosophy that you would bring to the nation's highest court. We need you to join us in a meaningful and important dialogue about the Constitution." U.S. Senate. Committee on the Judiciary. *Nomination of David H. Souter To Be Associate Justice of the Supreme Court of the United States.* Hearings, 101st Cong., 2d Sess., September 13,14,17&18, 1990. Washington, U.S. Govt. Print. Off., 1991. p. 2.

The Senate, Chairman Biden suggested, especially has a duty to determine a nominee's outlook and philosophy when the Court's "long-term direction is at stake, or at least in question." In his view, the Nation during the Souter hearings was at such a crossroad, because of "some very fundamental choices to be made "by the Court regarding the nature of protections provided by the first, Fourth, Fifth, Sixth and 14th Amendments of the Constitution. *Ibid.,*p.3.

[103] Kurtz, Howard. Judicial Reticence Frustrates Senators. *Washington Post,* September 9. 1986. p. A4.

thoroughness into the judicial philosophy of the nominee." For "the first time at any hearing in which a nominee has been seriously questioned about his views, no significant conflict arose over refusals to answer questions."[104] Later in 1987, after the Senate rejected the Bork nomination, a new Supreme Court nominee, Anthony M. Kennedy was asked, and responded to, numerous questions regarding his judicial philosophy, his view of past Supreme Court decisions, his method of constitutional interpretation, and his past rulings as a U.S. circuit court judge.[105] At his confirmation hearings in 1990, Supreme Court nominee David H. Souter, while declining to respond to questions regarding the constitutionality of a right to an abortion, deftly responded to questions on numerous other legal and constitutional issues. The nominee's performance as a whole, which Senator Biden (the chairman of the Judiciary Committee) called a "tour de force,"[106] overshadowed criticisms from some quarters about his unwillingness to discuss abortion rights.[107]

In September 1991, however, the refusal of Supreme Court nominee Clarence Thomas to answer various questions from Senators was a highly publicized aspect of the nominee's confirmation hearings. Judge Thomas declined to answer repeated questions about whether he believed in a fundamental right of women to choose an abortion (explaining each time that an answer would undermine his ability to sit impartially on a case raising the issue).[108] After his appearance, some Members on the Judiciary Committee complained, according to one news account, that the nominee "was being purposely vague and even disavowing his extensive record to win confirmation."[109]During Senate floor debate on the Thomas nomination, Senator Biden cited the "question of the adequacy of Judge Thomas's responses" to Judiciary Committee questions as one of his reasons for opposing the nomination. Senator Biden stressed that he was not referring to Judge Thomas's refusal to "to say how he would vote on Roe versus Wade"[110] but

[104] Ross, Questioning of Supreme Court Nominees, p. 123.

[105] See Cohodas, Nadine. Kennedy Hearings Indicate Easy Confirmation. *Congressional Quarterly Weekly Report,* v. 43, December 19, 1987. pp. 3129-33.

[106] Biskupic, Joan. Bush's Nominees Lack Baggage That Reagan's Often Carried. *Congressional Quarterly Weekly Report,* v. 48, September 22, 1990. p. 3019.

[107] See Biskupic, Joan. Souter Gains 13-1 Approval of Judiciary Committee. *Congressional Quarterly Weekly Report,* v. 48, September 29, 1990. pp. 3127-3128; Biskupic, Joan. Souter Confirmed Easily. *Congressional Quarterly Weekly Report,* v. 48, October 6, 1990. p. 32228.

[108] See, For example, Coyle, Marcia. They Hew to Script, with Some Ad-Libbing. *National law Journal,* v. 14, September 23, 1991. p. 8.

[109] Lewis, Neil A. Thomas Ends Testimony but Senators Grumble over Elusive Views. *New York Times,* September 17, 1991. p. A14.

[110] Senator Biden was referring to the landmark ruling *Roe v. Wade,* 410 U.S. 113 (1973), in which the Supreme Court found in the Constitution a right of privacy protecting a woman's decision whether or not to end a pregnancy.

rather to "the many constitutional issues, great, and small, contentious and settled, on which Judge Thomas declined to comment or made vague statements or provided unclear and uncertain distinctions."[111]

Another critic of Judge Thomas, Senator Daniel K. Inouye (D.-HI), suggested that the nominee's manner of responding to the Judiciary Committee was contrary to the purpose of having confirmation hearings:

> The ability to duck a question has gone from a sign of weakness to an art form. Rather than securing what I believe are simple answers to straightforward questions, my colleagues on the Judiciary Committee were trapped in a tangled web of evasion and skillful sidestepping. This cannot be what our Founding Fathers intended.[112]

A differing viewpoint, expressed by Senator Arlen Specter (R-PA), a member of the Judiciary Committee, was that Judge Thomas' responses to the Committee "were adequate." Senator Specter noted, for example, that the nominee had answered "detailed" questions on the establishment clause and free exercise clauses of the first Amendment, on *stare decisis,* on the right to privacy, and had been responsive to questions regarding the death penalty, equal protection cases, and affirmative action.[113] Relating Judge Thomas's responses to those of the two Supreme Court nominees immediately preceding him, Senator Specter remarked that Anthony M. Kennedy and David H. Souter, as well as Clarence Thomas, all answered "many questions." Even so, Senator Specter continued, the questioning process was not without its shortcomings:

> The process has evolved where it has a lot of similarities to the National Football League, where each team looks at the other's tapes before the Sunday game. We read Judge Thomas' writings, get an idea of him, and he looks at the tapes where we questioned other Justices in the past, and that highly stylized process has some real limitations. There is a dynamic quality, a certain dynamism of the hearings. And when nominees appear to feel safe,

---

[111] Biden, Joseph R., Jr. Opposition to the Confirmation of Clarence Thomas. Remarks in the Senate. *Congressional Record,* Daily Edition, v. 137, September 27, 1991. p. S13865.

[112] Inouye, Daniel k. Supreme Court of the United States. Remarks in the Senate. *Congressional Record,* Daily Edition, v. 137, October 3, 1991. p. S14285.

[113] Specter, Arlen. Supreme Court of the United States. Remarks in the Senate. *Congressional Record,* Daily Edition, v. 137, October 3, 1991. p. S14294. Senator Specter added that even "when he felt constrained – rightly in my view – not to answer a question because it required him to indicate how he would vote in a particular case, Judge Thomas gave the Judiciary Committee a sense of how he would approach such a case." *Ibid.*

> they answer fewer questions. If they feel they have to answer more questions to be confirmed, they do so.[114]

The ability of the nominee to decide when and how to respond to Committee questions was underscored more recently by Senator Biden, the chairman of the Judiciary Committee. In a June 25, 1992 floor speech on reform of the confirmation process, Senator Biden remarked:

> As I have said time and again, the choice about what questions to ask belongs to us on the committee. The choice about what questions to answer belongs to the nominee. Lacking any device of medieval inquisition, we have no way, as Senators, to make someone answer questions.[115]

Having said that, Senator Biden continued, he did not want "to undercut my string displeasure with what has happened to this aspect of the confirmation process since the Bork hearings." While Judge Bork "had a full and thorough exchange with the committee," and Judges Kennedy and Souter were "likewise fairly discursive in their answers to our questions," Judge Thomas decided that he would not "be as forthcoming" as Justices Kennedy and Souter had been and that "he did not need to use the hearings as an opportunity to explain his philosophy" as Judge Bork had tried to do. The result, Senator Biden maintained, was "what one of my colleagues called a version of a 'ritualized, Kabuki theater.'"[116]

Senator Biden declared that in the future it was important for the Senate to refocus the Supreme Court conformation process on the "judicial philosophy" of the nominee, "instead of on questions of his personal conduct." For this to occur, he said, the confirmation hearings of the Judiciary Committee "must be performed for full exploration of that philosophy." Noting that he had voted against Judge Thomas's confirmation "in part because of his evasiveness," Senator Biden said he would not "countenance any similar evasion on the part of any future nominees." The Senator then declared:

> In the future, I will be particularly rigorous in ensuring that every question I ask will be one that I believe a nominee should answer. And if the nominee declines to do so, I will — unless otherwise assured about a nominee's approach to the area in question — oppose that nominee.[117]

---

[114] *Ibid., p. S14291.*
[115] Biden, Reform of Confirmation Process (see footnote 18), p. S8865.
[116] *Ibid.*
[117] *Ibid.*

Like past Supreme Court nominees, future nominees who anticipate that they might have ideological difference with members of the Judiciary Committee can be expected to weigh which poses the greater danger to their confirmation — responding directly to Committee questions on sensitive issues, or declining to do so. Some political observers have speculated that Judge Thomas in 1991 perceived that responding guardedly to questions on such sensitive topics as abortion held fewer risks for him than did engaging with the Committee in "a forthright exchange of opinion about his past views."[118] By contrast, It has been suggested, Judge Bork in 1987, who already faced significant Judiciary Committee opposition to his nomination prior to his confirmation hearings, had little to lose and perhaps much to gain by replying without hesitation to Committee questions of a wide range of controversial issues.[119] In his June 1992 speech, announcing his intention to attach a high priority to the eliciting of direct replies from future nominees on their judicial philosophy, Chairman Biden added a new factor for any future nominee to weigh in deciding whether to be responsive to Committee questioning on sensitive topics.

Repetitiousness or Length of Questioning

Some critics of the Supreme Court confirmation process also have raised as an issue the repetitiousness or length of the interrogation that nominees must undergo at confirmation hearings. For example, during Senate floor debate on the Clarence Thomas nomination, Senator Orrin G. Hatch commented on the numerous questions about abortion that had been posed both to Judge Thomas and to the previous Supreme Court nominee, David H. Souter:

> Judge Souter, now Justice Souter, was asked 36 times about abortion; that was excessive. When I raised a fuss about it during Judge Thomas' testimony

---

118 Foe example, a *Wall Street Journal* editorial surmised that if Judge Thomas had "given the committee an opening on privacy, abortion, gender, and age discrimination or even economic liberties, they would have jumped him the way they did Robert Bork. It is only conjecture on our part, but we suspect that win or lose, he had come too far at this point in his life to let the particular members of this committee humiliate him in public." Clarence Thomas, P.O.W. *Wall Street Journal,* September 18, 1991. p. A14.

119 "Bork faced virulent opposition by large segments of the public and several leading committee members and testified at hearings that were among the most highly politicized in history. The only way for Bork to defuse the apparently potent opposition to his nomination seemed to be to try to clarify misconceptions about his philosophy and to explain his numerous controversial pronouncements on a host of subjects. Nominees whose records are less detailed or who face less intense opposition may well revert to the reticence which has characterized the testimony of past nominees." Ross, Questioning of Supreme Court Nominees (see footnote 99), p. 110, note 3.

in front of the committee, up to that point, Judge Thomas had been queried about abortion 67 times. And by the end of the hearings, it was up to around 100 times, which is triple the number of times Justice Souter was asked.[120]

The number of questions posed to Judge Thomas about abortion during the confirmation hearings also drew criticism from Senator John C. Danforth of Missouri:

> I have not made a count of how many times he was asked from beginning to end, but it was surely more than 70. Was it 80, 90, 100?
>
> Mr. President, when do we move beyond an honest inquiry into a person's views and badgering somebody? Is it after the first five questions, or 10, or 20, or 50 or 60 or 70?[121]

The circumstance, during confirmation hearings, of being watched by millions of television viewers (many of them constituents), some have maintained, is a temptation for Senators to ask more questions than are necessary. Two legal scholars, for example, are critical of "the current emphasis on a process that has become a public spectacle"; they have suggested among the possible remedies that "there should be sharp time limits on senatorial questioning."[122] Another scholar on the Supreme Court confirmation process has recommended that the Judiciary Committee "generally cut down on the number of rounds" that Members are allowed for questioning of the nominee.[123]

Certain arguments, however, might be raised against sharply cutting back the opportunities for Senators to questions Supreme Court nominees at confirmation hearings. If recent past experience is a reliable guide, a nominee can be expected to be questioned for more than three days only if he or she is notably controversial.[124] In such an event, it can be argued, any negative effects of

---

[120] Hatch, Orrin G. Supreme Court of the United States. Remarks in the Senate. *Congressional Record,* Daily Edition, v. 137, October 3, 1991. p. S14305.

[121] Danforth, John C. Supreme Court of the United States. Remarks in the Senate. *Congressional Record,* Daily Edition, v. 137, October 3, 1991. p. 14288.

[122] Strauss and Sunstein, Seant4e and Constitution (see footnote 95), pp. 1519-20.

[123] Abraham, Henry J., James Hart Professor of Government and Foreign Affairs, University of Virginia. Telephone interview. Charlottesville, Virginia, June 4, 1992.

[124] During the Reagan and Bush Residencies, only two Supreme Court nominees testified before the Senate Judiciary Committee for more than three days – in 1987, Robert Bork, for five days; and in 1991, Clarence Thomas, for five days, during the first round of hearings on his nominations, and than again, for two days, during a second set of hearings held on allegations that he had once engaged in sexual harassment of a colleague. The testimony and questioning for the other Supreme Court nominees during this period involved the following number of days: Sandra Day O'Connor (1981), three days; William H. Rehnquist (1986), two days; Antonin Scalia (1986), one day; Anthony M. Kennedy (1987), two days; David H. Souter (1990), three days.

protracted interrogation, such as repetitiousness, would be offset by the benefits of fully exploring the controversies associated with the nomination through direct engaging of the nominee. It would seem difficult to prescribe a tome limit, in number of days or rounds of questioning, for Supreme Court nominations in general, since the amount of time that would appear to be needed by the judiciary Committee for questioning would almost surely vary from one nomination to another.

Any effort to impose limits on repetitious questioning also could be expected to encounter problems. At any given hearing, a Senator might argue that it is necessary to pose questions already asked by another Senator in order to create a context for more probing questions or for a line of questioning in a new but associated area; or that his or her questions, while quite similar to earlier questions, involve slightly different nuances the importance of which will be demonstrated as questioning proceeds. It would also be awkward for the Committee Chairman — or a voting majority in the Committee — to stop a line of questioning because of repetitiousness; such situations in all likelihood would involve embarrassment to the interrogating Member and detract attention from the Committee's immediate concern, the qualifications of the nominee.

In rebuttal, the preceding arguments do not necessarily invalidate the case that questioning at confirmation hearings can, if not restrained, become too repetitive or protracted, reflecting badly on the Committee. Accordingly, it might be argued that the Committee, in preparation for the next Supreme Court confirmation hearing, could address the issue of whether new time limitations are called for or whether the Committee's members should try to avoid repetitious questioning.

When Hearings Should be Closed

The October 10-13, 1991 hearings on Professor Anita Hill's sexual harassment allegations against Clarence Thomas generated much follow-up discussion as to when confirmation hearings should be closed to the public. Senate Rule XXVI.5(b) provides that Senate committee meetings, including hearings, shall be open to the public, except that a committee may vote in open session by a majority to close a meeting if matters to be discussed or testimony will, among other things,

> ...tend to charge individual with crime or misconduct, to disgrace or injure the professional standing of an individual, or otherwise to expose an

individual to public contempt or obloquy, or will represent a clearly unwarranted invasion of the privacy of an individual.[125]

Although the rule language clearly would have permitted the Committee to consider the Hill allegations in closed session, various factors militated against this option. Perhaps foremost was the fact that the allegations, which Professor Hill initially had communicated on a confidential basis to both the Committee and the Federal Bureau of Investigation, had subsequently been leaked anonymously and then made public in the press on October 6, 1991. With Senate and public attention, as a result of media reports, focused on the Hill allegations, the Senate on October 8 agreed by unanimous consent to reschedule its October 9 vote on the Thomas nomination for October 15, in order, in the words of the Senate Majority Leader, "to give time for further inquiry into this matter by the Judiciary Committee."[126] Besides the call by various Members of the Senate for public hearings, other circumstances seemed to dictate an open hearings approach, according to *Congressional Quarterly Weekly Report.* The journal reported that, due to the fact that "Hill's charges has become public through a leak and the nation's newspapers were questioning whether the Senate was trying to cover up a serious charge, a closed hearing was virtually impossible."[127] Also highly relevant, as the hearings began, was that Chairman Biden invited any witness to request a private session. Yet, as one Committee Member observed, during "those three marathon days of hearings, not one witness accepted that invitation."[128]

The openness of the Hill/Thomas hearings, nonetheless, would itself prove highly controversial, with the Committee faulted by many for eliciting vivid, lurid testimony about a nominee's alleged misconduct seen and heard by the public at

---

125 U.S. Congress. Senate. *Standing Rules of the Senate; Revised to March 1, 1990.* Senate Document No. 101-25, 101st Cong., 2d Sess. Washington, U.S. Govt. Print. Off., 1990. p. 37. Rule XXVI5.(b) also provides that committees may vote to close meetings if the matters to be discussed or testimony to be taken would disclose national defense secrets, relate solely to internal committee matters, disclose the secret identity of law enforcement agents, disclose trade secrets, or might divulge other matters required under the law to be kept confidential. *Ibid.*

126 Mitchell, George J. Unanimous Consent Agreement. Remarks in the Senate. *Congressional Record,* Daily Edition, v. 137, October 8, 1991. p. S.14566.

127 Biskupic, Joan. A Process Under Scrutiny. *Congressional Quarterly Weekly Report,* v. 49, October 19, 1991. p. 3031. A member of the Judiciary Committee, Senator Dennis DeConcini, offered a similar assessment, in retrospect, of the untenability of holding the Hill/Thomas hearings in closed session. The "reality of the matter," he wrote, was "that once the public became aware of the allegation, the Senate risked the accusation of a cover-up if subsequent investigative hearings were held in closed meetings." DeConcini, Examining the Process (see footnote 27), p. 21.

128 DeConcini, Examining the Process (see footnote 27), p. 22.

large.[129] On October 16, 1991, the day after the Senate's confirmation of Clarence Thomas to the Supreme Court, Senator Sam Nunn (D-GA) criticized the Senate for having "succumbed to a momentary desire to accommodate the public's right to know" about Professor Hill's confidential allegations. "The result of indulging this momentary desire," Senator Nunn asserted, has — in [Alexander] Hamilton's prophetic phrase — terminated in 'general distress, dissatisfaction, and disgust.'"[130] The Senator declared it to be vital that information concerning the private lives of individuals be considered on closed session whenever possible. He added:

> Is not always possible, but insofar as possible that should be the driving rule. Public airing of every allegation about a nominee can cause long-term damage to a nominee's reputation, even if it is totally refuted. Even if totally refuted, the damage is very serious.[131]

A similar perspective was offered by Lloyd N. Cutler, a Washington lawyer and former White House counsel in the Carter Administration. In a commentary in the *Washington Post,* Mr. Cuter urged that when "a charge of personal misconduct is made, especially sexual misconduct and the responsible Senate committee decides that the charge is substantial enough to require an evidentiary hearing, the committee should invoke Senate Rule XXV1.5(b) and conduct the hearing in a secret executive session."[132] While conceding that "what happens behind closed doors might leak out anyway," Mr. Cutler said a leak would be preferable to open hearings. Among other things, the leak "could only be of the committee report, or of second hand accounts of who said what at the hearing or on the Senate floor. There would be no videotape to be televised in vivid sound and pictures."[133]

---

[129] See, for example, Garrett, Major. Hearings Scar Image of Senate. *Washington Times,* October 20, 1991. pp. A1,A6; Balz, Dan. Thomas Hearings Resonate Across U.S. *Washington Post,* October 17, 1991. pp. A1,A10.

[130] Nunn, Sam. Proceedings Concerning the Nomination of Judge Clarence Thomas To Be an Associate Justice of the U.S. Supreme Court. Remarks in the Senate. *Congressional Record,* Daily Edition, v. 137, October 16, 1991. p. S14726.

[131] *Ibid.,* p. S14727.

[132] Cutler, Lloyd N. Why Not Executive Sessions? *Washington Post,* October 17, 1991. p. A23. "After the hearing, the committee should file a report with the full Senate summarizing the gist of the testimony and any committee findings and conclusions on the issue. In the discretion of the committee, the report would be published and debate on the Senate floor would be in open session, or the report itself would be secret and would be presented to the full Senate in executive session." *Ibid.*

[133] *Ibid.* If "a leak occurred, we would still better off than now "for other reasons as well, according to Mr. Cutler. He listed the following:

Shortly thereafter, on October 24, 1991, Senator Dennis DeConcini proposed amending paragraph 5(b) of Senate Rule XXVI. That paragraph, as noted above, provides for *open* Senate committee meetings, unless a committee votes to close a meeting, for any one of six enumerated reasons of sensitivity-among them, the reason that an open meeting would tend to "disgrace or injure the professional standing of an individual." Senator DeConcini stated he disagreed "with the presumption, contained in the rules, that requires these sensitive matters to be aired in public unless a majority of committee or subcommittee members determine that a closed session is preferable."[134] The Senator proposed changing the presumption of paragraph 5(b) so that it would be in favor of *closed* committee sessions if any of the six enumerated sensitive matters applied.[135] He noted that S. Res 206, which he had just introduced, would effect that change. Thus, if the Deconcini resolution were adopted, a Judiciary Committee meeting held to consider misconduct allegations against a Supreme Court nominee would be conducted in *closed* session, *unless* a majority of the members of the Committee determined by recorded vote to open the meeting to the public.[136]

A few months later, a less automatic approach to closing confirmation hearings would be prescribed by the Senate Democratic Task Force on the Confirmation Process. The Task Force's report stressed "the public's right to know" as an important consideration counter-balancing the nominee's "right to privacy":

- "The hearing would be much shorter and to the point. Deprived of their 12-camera TV studio and their national audience of millions, senators would waste much less time in irrelevant discourses on their own sensitivity and thoughtfulness and could concentrate on developing the facts.
- "The accuser and the accused would suffer less humiliation and invasion of their privacy than a televised public hearing entails.
- "The Senate would avoid confirming the prevalent low public opinion of those we have elected to high office.
- "The circus atmosphere of last weekend would not be repeated, and the standards of what can be said on daylight television to family audiences would not fall even lower than they are today."

[134] DeConcini, Dennis. Senate resolution 206 – Amending the Standing Rules of the Senate. Remarks in the Senate. *Congressional Record,* Daily Edition, v. 137, October 24, 1991. p. S15203.

[135] Senator DeConcini said he believed this amendment would "protect sensitive individual and Government interests and ultimately protect the Senate's confirmation and investigation process from sensationalized exposure than can cause irreparable harm." *Ibid.*

[136] Specifically, S. Res. 206 provided that paragraph 5(b) be amended so that its requirement of open committee meetings and hearings be followed by the following clause: "except that a meeting or series of meetings to discuss matters enumerated in clauses (1) through (6) shall be conducted in closed session unless a majority of the Members of the committee or subcommittee determine, by a recorded vote, that the meeting or hearing should be open to the public." *Ibid.*

> The confirmation process must carefully balance the nominee's right to privacy against the public's right to Know, with any curtailment of the latter approached cautiously. Unlike the Executive Branch's closed process for selecting nominees, the Senate's confirmation hearings are the only aspect of the appointment process open to the public.[137]

Further, the Task Force maintained, "While the nominee's right to privacy is important, the public's right to know must be zealously guarded."[138]

Sounding a cautionary note, the Task Force recommended that the Standing Rules of the Senate "should be applied carefully in determining whether to conduct a closed hearing. In instances where testimony is likely to involve allegations that could invade and injure the reputation of a nominee, a committee should consider a closed session when a *nominee* so requests."[139] (Emphasis added)

Subsequently, however, one of the Task Force's five members, Senator Biden, declared a new policy for the Judiciary Committee. Senator Biden declared his intention in the future, as Chairman of the Committee, to provide for a closed investigative hearing as a matter of course for Supreme Court nominees. In June, 25, 1992 floor remarks on the Supreme Court confirmation process, Senator Biden discussed his reform and the reasons for it:

> ...because, ultimately, the question with respect to investigations of a Supreme Court nominee is the credibility and character of that nominee, in the future, ...as long as I am chairman, the committee will routinely conduct a closed session with each nominee to ask that nominee — face-to-face, on the record, under oath — about all investigative charges against that person.
>
> This hearing will be conducted in all cases, even where there are no major investigative issues to be resolved, so that the holding of such a

[137] Democratic Task force, Report (see footnote 14), p. S898. A similar position on this issue, weighing the interests of privacy against the public's right to know, was taken by an ad hoc committee of the Now York City Bar Association: "When the nominee is charged with misconduct that implicates not only issues of personal ethics, but also substantial privacy concerns (whether those of the candidate, an accuser or a witness), the Judiciary Committee should carefully weight those concerns and the desire to preserve the legitimacy and dignity of the process, on the one hand, against the significant value of unfettered public access to the hearings, on the other hand, to determine whether a closed session is appropriate." NYC Bar Association, *Report* (see footnote 60), p. 4.

[138] *Ibid.*

[139] *Ibid.* By contrast, neither the Cutler proposal nor S. Res. 206, above, identified a nominee's request for closed hearings as a precondition for closing a hearing.

hearing cannot be taken to demonstrate that the committee has received adverse confidential information about the nominee.[140]

This now procedure, Senator Biden acknowledged, could be criticized. He added, however, that "there are no easy answers when questions of fairness, thoroughness, civil liberties, and the future of the Court collide under the glaring klieg lights of television cameras."[141] While instituting, as a regular procedure, a closed hearing for each Supreme Court nominee on any investigative charges against that person, Senator Biden did not discuss, and hence did not rule out, the option of also holding an open hearing on such charges afterwards, if circumstances seemed to warrant this.

An Impartial Inquiry or an Adversary Proceeding?

During and after Senate consideration of the Clarence Thomas nomination, many observers expressed concerns about what they perceived to be the politicized nature of Supreme Court confirmation hearings. They felt that the Thomas hearings in September and October of 1991 had become too adversarial, and that the Judiciary Committee in the future should collectively make a greater effort to conduct an impartial inquiry into the qualifications of Supreme Court nominees. Others, however, suggested that, particularly if a nomination appears to be a partisan political act, expectations of impartiality within the Committee are unrealistic and that Committee members shouldn't pretend otherwise, but rater should proceed openly in an adversary fashion when important political issues appear to be at stake.

President Bush was prominent among those advocating that confirmation hearings become less politicized and polarized. In an October 24, 1991 speech, the president referred disapprovingly to the hearings held earlier that month on sexual harassment allegations which Anita Hill had made against Clarence Thomas. President Bush declared that the "bruising hearings showed what happens when political factions let agendas overwhelm personal decency," adding a few moments later that "we must promote more tolerant, less viciously partisan debate."[142]

---

[140] "The transcripts of that session," senator Biden added, "will be part of the confidential record of the nomination made available, with the FBI report, to all Senators." Biden, Reform of Confirmation Process (see footnote), p. S8866.

[141] *Ibid.*

[142] Bush, Remarks to Public Administration Groups (see footnote 63), p. 1497.

Others expressed similar criticisms. During Senate floor debate on the Thomas nomination, Senator Mark O. Hatfield remarked, "It is now almost an adversarial relationship between the nominees and the committee. In my opinion, this is part of the reflection of divided Government that we have today."[143] From academia, one legal scholar wrote that the "present form or committee proceedings on adversary party lines, in which the primary objective appears to be to defeat the other side at all costs, should be abandoned."[144] Subsequently the Senate Democratic Task Force on the Confirmation Process indicated that it, too, looked with disfavor upon adversary proceedings as a model for confirmation hearings. "Confirmation hearings," the Task Force said in its report, "are not adversarial proceedings; they are part of the Senate's exercise of a constitutionally-mandated duty. They should consist of a productive exchange of views."[145]

Concerns over confirmation hearing becoming too adversarial have prompted a wide variety of proposed remedial measures. Some already have been discussed in these report, such as proposals to institute more significant consultation between the Senate and president in the nominee selection process or to close hearings when there are serious allegations against a nominee; another relevant reform proposal, to delegate all or some of the questioning during hearings to non-Senate Members, will be discussed below. All of these proposals are based in part on a perceived need to reduce the degree of partisanship or acrimony in the hearings phase or other phases of the confirmation process.[146]

Some observers, however, have questioned whether political impartiality can be practiced at Supreme Court confirmation hearings, especially if a nominee is controversial or has been accused of wrongdoing. The Judiciary Committee, in the view of one legal scholar, is placed in a particularly awkward position when it has to function as an impartial "jury," which he maintains was the operating standard

---

[143] Hatfield, Mark O. Nomination of Clarence Thomas, of Georgia, To Be an Associate Justice of the Supreme Court of the United States. *Congressional Record,* Daily Edition, v. 137, October 3, 1991. p. S14323.

[144] Forrester, Call for Integrity (see footnote 28), p. 19. See also comment of University of Chicago law professor Michael W. McConnell on what he perceived as the role of Judiciary Committee members, depending on their party affiliation, to either defend the "innocence" of Clarence Thomas "up until the point it became untenable," or to "go on the offensive." Goldberg, Stephanie B. "What's the Alternative?: A Roundtable on the Confirmation Process. *ABA Journal,* v. 78, January 1992. p. 45.

[145] Task Force, Report (see footnote14), p. S896.

[146] Another possible reform to reduce partisan politics at Supreme Court confirmation hearings, identified by one scholar, would be to reconstitute the membership of the Senate Judiciary Committee to have the same number of Democrats and Republicans. Abraham, Henry J. James Hart Professor of Government and Foreign Affairs, University of Virginia. Telephone interview, Charlottesville, Virginia, June 4, 1992.

for the Committee during the second round of Thomas hearings in October 1991 (when the Committee focused on the Hill allegations). The effort on the Committee's part to create an air of impartiality, in this scholar's view, was actually harmful. He explained:

> The trial-like atmosphere was not only fake or disingenuous; it had powerful, and harmful, effects that shifted the focus of the hearing in important ways. First, the seeming procedural regularity and apparent role definition camouflaged to some extent the intensely political nature of the event. ...The due process overtones... offered a pretense of fairness that was easy to manipulate and to exploit. Clarence Thomas's supporters were able both to characterize the charges as "unfair" and yet to demand strict procedural rules in the name of fairness. His opponents were caught in their effort to maintain an appearance of neutrality. Locked into their juror –judge roles, they never really carried out any semblance of a genuine investigation of the allegations. The confusion of roles and the effort to assume the mantle of judicial fairness prevented the Senate from doing what it sometimes can do, with varying degrees of success: investigate.[147]

Another scholar, in a similar vein, has suggested that diverging "political goals" associated with the two-party composition of the Judiciary Committee confound efforts to foster a non-adversary environment:

> The divergence in political goals and objectives is easily kept in view when the topic is substantive legislation, but it gets lost at moments like Hill/Thomas, when the popular perception is that the Senate "as an institution" has come under attack. Yet to speak about "the Committee" or "the Senate" as having a collective interest in restoring trust on government falsely assumes that Democrats and Republicans benefit equally from such trust. While almost all politicians want to keep their jobs, "the institution" needs to work in very different ways for it to satisfy the political objectives of the two parties.[148]

[147] Curtis, Dennis E. The Fake Trial. *Southern California Law Review,* v. 65, May 1992. p. 1525. An introductory note identifies the author as Robert C. and Nanette T. Packard Professor of Clinical Legal Education, University of Southern California Law Center. Also, in that note, the author states: "I provided some assistance to Anita Hill's advisors during the hearings; I acknowledge that I am biased in her favor." *Ibid.*, p. 1523.

[148] Schroeder, Christopher H. Congress Stories. *Southern California Law Review,* v. 65, May 1992. p. 1564. The author is identified in an introductory note as a Professor of Law at Duke University School of Law. Also, in the introductory note, the author states: "In various capacities, I have worked for the Chairman of the Senate Judiciary Committee, Joseph R. Biden, Jr., during the Senate's consideration of Supreme Court nominees Robert Bork, Anthony Kennedy, David Souter, and Clarence Thomas. In order to disclose relevant biases, I need also to say that I have deep respect for Senator Biden as a man of integrity and honor." *Ibid.*, p. 1531.

This analysis, like the preceding scholar's, came in the context of the Hill/Thomas hearings; nonetheless, it could be argued that the political factors he cited would be as relevant to almost any confirmation hearing involving a controversial Supreme Court nomination.

Subsequently, Senator Biden also questioned the notion that Senators should be politically neutral in assessing a Supreme Court nominee. In a June 25, 1992 floor speech, the Judiciary Committee Chairman commented that the Supreme Court confirmation process "has been infected by the general meanness and nastiness that pervades our political process today."[149] Senator Biden said the "root cause" of this problem and, more generally, of the "current collapse or the confirmation process," was "the [Bush] administration's campaign to make the Supreme Court an agent of an ultraright conservative social agenda which lacks support in the Congress and in the country."[150]If it appears that a nominee may have an ideological agenda, or may promote such an agenda if confirmed to the Court, it is entirely proper, Senator Biden indicated, for members of the Judiciary Committee who disagree with that agenda to make a political decision about the nominee. Senator Biden declared:

> Confirmation hearings are not trials, We are not a court we are a legislative body. They are congressional hearings. Senators are not judges. We are Senators. Our decision on a nominee is not a neutral ruling as a judge would render. It is, as the Constitution designed it, a political choice about values and philosophy.[151]

Further, Senator Biden asserted, it is proper for Senators to make a political decision of this sort, even before a nominee's confirmation hearings. Senators who take "early stands" on nominees, he said, should not refrain from discussing the nomination prior to confirmation hearings, but rather should engage in a "debate by principles about real issues" and about the philosophy of the nominee. Nonparticipation by Senators in such pre-hearings debate, Senator Biden maintained, creates a "vacuum," which is "filled by pundits, lobbying groups, interest groups, ideological fringes," allowing them "to define the debate and dictat[e] the tactics."[152]

Hence, Senator Biden's speech echoed the theme, expressed earlier by many others, that the debate over Supreme Court nominations has become too rancorous and adversarial. At the same time, the speech was distinctive in also suggesting

---

[149] Biden, Reform of Confirmation Process (see footnote 18), p. S8861.
[150] *Ibid.*, p. S8860.
[151] *Ibid.*, p. S8864.

that the tone of debate over controversial Supreme Court nominations would be elevated, and made less bitter, if Senators themselves engaged more actively in debate about the nominees' philosophy prior to confirmation hearings.[153]

Procedures for Receiving Evidence Concerning Alleged Misconduct

Another object for proposed reform has been the specific procedures to be followed by the Senate Judiciary Committee when it hears or otherwise receives evidence concerning alleged misconduct by a Supreme Court nominee. Common to such proposals is an express or implied concern for insuring the fairness and effectiveness of the Committee's inquiry-whether it be conducted in private or public session, or by Committee members or others specially trained to receive evidence.

Various proposals of this sort were made in the wake of the Senate's confirmation of Clarence Thomas. One legal commentator, for instance, recommended that prospective witnesses as well as the Supreme Court nominee be required to answer questions in writing under oath *before* the holding of hearings. Then, at "the slightest indication of financial, sexual or other misdeeds, or allegations about the nominee's integrity, character or credibility, all such procedures should be examined in closed session, and on a vote of the committee thereafter, a decision could be made whether to air the matter publicly."[154]

Another observer maintained that allegations of "immoral or criminal behavior by presidential appointments ought to be handled with special care." He urged the creation of "a procedure for the evaluation of such charges in closed proceedings," with a "distinguished investigator appointed from outside the Senate" to preside over the proceedings.[155] Concern for procedural reform was also expressed by a legal scholar who proposed that investigation and interrogation of Supreme Court nominees and witnesses be conducted by an

---

[152] *Ibid.*

[153] Disagreeing with Senator Biden in this point, an editorial in the *Washington Times* contended: "Rather than de-politicizing the process, 'early' opposition means that future nominees will face the kind of restrained objectivity that met the nomination of Judge Robert Bork." Sen. Biden's New Rules. *Washington Times,* July 8, 1992. p. G2.

[154] Nellis, Imperfect Proceeding (see footnote 36), p. 16.

[155] "A procedure such as this would spare us the most offensive feature of the Thomas hearings: the spectacle of a television 'trial' in which the painstaking work of sorting through testimony is upstaged by the posturing of politicians. Witnesses could be heard and examined at length by an investigator with allegiance to neither side in a partisan confirmation hearing." Gerety, Tom. Fine-Tuning 'Advice and Consent.' *Chicago Tribune.* October 29, 1991. Sec. 1, p. 15. The author is identified as a constitutional scholar and the and the president of Trinity College in Hartford, Connecticut.

independent counsel; under this arrangement, a nonpartisan chairman of a special commission would "preside with impartiality and authority in the basis *of rules and procedures carefully crafted by experts beforehand.*"[156] (Emphasis added)

Reform of the rules governing committee receipt of information before and during Supreme Court confirmation hearings has also been proposed by an ad hoc committee of the Now York City Bar Association. In a June 1992 report, the bar association committee, among other things, concluded that:

> The fairness and effectiveness of the judiciary Committee's fact-finding function can be enhanced via: (a) the establishment of firm deadlines after which new information, evidence and charges concerning the nominee will not be received or considered absent extraordinary circumstances; (b) the provision of sufficient opportunity for the presentation of expert witness, rebuttal and sur-rebuttal testimony on the hearing of issues of disputed fact; and (c) the use of rules of evidence to exclude inadmissible hearsay, allegations that are unsubstantiated, and testimony that is without foundation.[157]

As noted earlier,[158] Chairman Biden on June 25, 1992 announced a new procedure, under which the Judiciary Committee will hold a closed investigative hearing for every future Supreme Court nominee as a matter of course — even, the Chairman observed, "when there are no major investigative issues to be resolved." Under this arrangement, the Committee over the long term presumably will develop a standard set of special procedures that will be followed in each closed door session. In turn, regular experience in using such procedures, it could be argued, might better enable the Committee to inquire into any serious accusations filed against a future Supreme Court nominee with less of a sense of crisis than was experienced during the Hill-Thomas episode.

Another procedural concern to some has been the speed with which the Senate Judiciary Committee and the Senate as a whole should act when an allegation of misconduct has been made against a Supreme Court nominee. A lesson of the Anita Hill/Clarence Thomas hearings, according to one member of the Judiciary Committee, was that when "serious charge is made about a Supreme

---

156 Forrester, Call for Integrity (see footnote 28), p. 19.

157 NYC Bar Association, *Report* (see footnote 60), p. 5. The committee also recommended that the Judiciary Committee seriously consider "the use of special independent counsel to conduct the examination of the nominee and witnesses in special hearings held to determine the truth of specific allegations... made against the nominee." *Ibid.*, p. 4.

158 See remarks of Senator Biden in earlier section of this report under the heading "When Hearings Should Be Closed." See also Biden, Reform of Confirmation Process (see footnote 18), p. S8866.

Court nominee, Committee hearings should not be rushed." this view was expressed by Senator Paul Simon of Illinois, who pointed to the fact that the Senate's vote to confirm Clarence Thomas on October 15, 1991 occurred within days of the Judiciary Committee's hearings on Professor Anita Hill's allegation against the nominee. Following those hearings, Senator Simon has asserted, "We should have delayed, giving us time to hear a limited number of additional witnesses giving the Senators and the public a chance to let the dust settle, to perhaps make a more rational decision."[159]

Questioning Conducted by Non-Members

Some also have proposed that the Senate Judiciary Committee delegate part or all of its members' questioning duties at confirmation hearings to specially trained lawyers. Such a step, it has been argued, would be particularly helpful when the Committee's primary objective is to determine the truth in a factual dispute — which was the principal purpose of the Committee's hearings in October 1991 on sexual harassment allegations made by Anita Hill against Clarence Thomas.

During and after the Hill/Thomas hearings, a well-publicized frustration of many Members on the Committee and in the Senate as a whole was the inability to determine with any certainty who was telling the truth — the nominee or his accuser. After the fact, various observers in the legal community questioned the Committee's reliance on its own members to conduct all of the questioning of judge Thomas, Professor Hill and the other witnesses during the hearings. Illustrative was the assessment of one attorney who has served as counsel to numerous House and Senate committees:

> People whose opinions I respect argue that the process of Senate hearings would be fairer if experienced lawyers representing the majority and minority of the committee were permitted to ask all fact-finding questions. The senators would follow up. I am familiar with this method, since it was used by Senator Estes Kefauver [D-TN] when I was counsel to the Senate Organized Crime Committee in 1950-'52. There is much to be said for the

[159] Simon, Paul *Advice & Consent*. Washington, National Press Books, Inc., 1992. p. 305. (Hereafter cited as Simon, *Advice & Consent)* Senator Simon quoted two other Members of the Judiciary Committee who expressed sentiments similar to his about the speed which the senate acted on the Thomas nomination. *Ibid.*, p. 306.

proposal; lawyers would be less likely to politicize the process, especially in closed session.[160]

The use of outside counsel with special cross-examining skills, some argued, would be especially helpful to the Committee when it is concerned with determining the credibility of hearing witnesses. I this vein, noted defense attorney F. Lee Bailey declared emphatically that "[a]ny time a Senate committee confronts a serious credibility clash in an important inquiry... and *declines* to bring in experienced cross-examiners, its chair should state for the record which of its designated members is so expert in this undertaking that outside help is not needed."[161]

An independent counsel, it has been contended, particularly can perform a service during an investigation into "specific charges of ethical or legal wrongdoing that are denied by the nominee. "Marking this recommendation, an ad hoc committee of the New York City Bar Association maintained that such an investigation differs "qualitatively from typical confirmation hearings, and more resembles a trial." Hence, the committee maintained:

> ...questioning by independent counsel with significant trial experience would be especially useful. The notion that the Senate will not be willing to relinquish its principal questioning role seems less applicable in this context: as the Thomas hearings indicated, when the relevant charges generate intense public controversy and division, and involve issues of ethical impropriety the public spotlight might be too intense for at least some Senators and, indeed, might constrain them from asking all of the questions that need to be asked in the interests of truth and fairness. In any event, the Senators would be free to supplement independent counsels' inquiry with questions of their own.[162]

---

[160] Nellis, Imperfect Proceeding (see footnote 36), p. 16. Mr. Nellis, the article notes, recently had been general counsel to the House Judiciary Committee.
Expressing a somewhat similar view, Duke University law professor Walter Dellinger has commented that "staff counsel doesn't have to worry as much as senators about maintaining an appearance of impartiality or about asking questions that are potentially politically embarrassing." Goldberg, What's the Alternative? (see footnote 91), p. 45.
See also, Forrester, Call for Integrity (see footnote 28), p. 19, in which the author declares: "The investigation and ultimate interrogation of the nominee and the witnesses should be conducted by independent counsel of proven integrity and ability who would pose well-prepared questions to the witnesses, questions that would be brief, to the point, and fair." Professor Forrester would further minimize the involvement of Judiciary Committee Members when a Supreme Court nominee is accused of wrongdoing; the Senate, in that case, "should delegate its investigatory and fact-finding process to a blue ribbon commission composed of esteemed citizens devoted to the general welfare, rather than to party politics." *Ibid.*

[161] Bailey, F. Lee. Where Was the Crucible? The Cross-Examination That Wasn't. *ABA Journal,* v. 78, January 1992. p. 49.

[162] NYC Bar Association, *Report* (see footnote 60), pp. 24-25.

Other observers have proposed that lawyers with special skills or knowledge be used to conduct questioning not only relating to factual but also to legal and constitutional issues. Suggesting that perhaps some of the questioning in the latter areas be done by outside counsel, two scholars note that "Senators have an extraordinary range of duties. Although many Senators are, by training and temperament, well equipped to handle constitutional issues, it is unreasonable to expect members of the Judiciary Committee to be specialists in the intricacies of legal doctrine."[163]

Such proposals as the above, however, failed to receive the endorsement of the Senate Democratic Task Force on the Confirmation Process. Instead, the Task Force left to each Senate committee the determination of whether and when to use counsels to conduct questioning at confirmation hearings. In a report to the Senate Majority Leader, the Task Force expressed the following position on the issue:

> The duty of reviewing a nominee's qualifications should remain with the Members of the Senate. Senators have the unique qualifications and historical perspective to put nominee's answers in their proper context, based on prior confirmation hearings in which those Senators have participated. The Task Force considered recommending that all committees use committee counsel to conduct the questioning of nominees at confirmation hearings and rejected that option. Current rules permit committees to give their legal counsel a more active role in a committee hearing, including a confirmation process. The determination to use committee counsel should be made by the respective committees, based on their unique needs and circumstances.[164]

The ad hoc committee distinguished using an *independent* counsel (which it recommended) from "entrusting all or some of the questioning to special *majority* and *minority* counsel" (which it rejected). The latter individuals, the committee maintained, "would presumably act at the specific direction of the Senators from each party, and thereby offer little improvement in the content and approach of the inquiry. Moreover, vesting the authority to question in counsel representing each party would have the undesirable effect of explicitly condoning – indeed, institutionalizing – a view of the process as essentially, if not exclusively , partisan." *Ibid.*, p. 23.

[163] Strauss and Sunstein, Senate and Constitution (see footnote 95), p. 1519. The article notes that the two authors are both law professors at the University of Chicago and that Professor Strauss "served as Special Counsel to the United States Senate Committee on the Judiciary in connection with the nomination of Justice David H. Souter to the Supreme Court." *Ibid.*, p. 1491.

[164] Democratic Task Force, Report (see footnote 14), p. S896.

Involvement of Outside Interest Groups

Various proposed reforms also would affect the role which outside groups play in the nomination and confirmation process. Attention in this area has focused not only on the activities of overtly partisan interest groups which typically take a stand in favor of or against a Supreme Court nominee soon after the nomination is announced. The reform debate also has touched on the longstanding quasi-governmental role of the American Bar Association in rating the qualifications of Supreme Court nominees.

Role of the ABA Standing Committee on the Federal Judiciary

The proper role to be played by the American Bar Association in evaluating Supreme Court nominees has been a recurring issue in recent years.

Since 1948 the ABA's Standing Committee on the Federal Judiciary has, at the request of the Senate Judiciary Committee, evaluated the qualifications of persons considered for appointment to the Supreme Court, the U.S. Circuit Courts of Appeals, and the U.S. District Courts. Since 1952 the Standing Committee has performed the same service for the President and the Justice Department.[165] The historical reasons for formally involving the ABA in the nomination process were noted by Chairman Biden of the Judiciary Committee in a 1989 hearing:

> ...The collective wisdom some 40 years age was that [1] the selection of Federal judges relied too heavily on political patronage [2] cronyism, not competence, was all too often the reason for selecting a political nominee, and [3] depoliticizing the nominating process was thought to be essential. To help insure that only the highest caliber men and women ascended to the bench, the ABA was asked to come in and make recommendations.[166]

The stated objective of the Standing Committee in investigating a Supreme Court nominee is to acquire information on his or her professional competence, integrity, and temperament.[167] The basic procedures employed by the Standing

---

165 *The ABA Standing Committee on Federal Judiciary: What It Is and How It Works.* American Bar Association, 1991. p. 2. Hereafter cited as ABA, *Standing Committee.*

166 U.S. Congress. Committee on the Judiciary. *The ABA in the Judiciary Nomination Process.* Hearing on the Role of the American Bar Association in the Judicial Evaluation Process, 101st Cong., 1st Sess, June 2, 1989. Washington, U.S. Govt. Print. Off., 1991. p. 2.

167 "The Committee's process is structured to achieve impartial evaluations of the integrity, professional competence and judicial temperament of prospective nominees for the judiciary. The Committee's goal is to support and encourage the selection of the best qualified persons for the federal judiciary." ABA, *Standing Committee, p.2.*

Committee in this investigation are the following: Interviews are conducted throughout the country of individuals thought likely to have information regarding the nominee's fitness to serve on the Court. This undertaking may involve hundreds of interviews. [168] Also, the legal writing of the nominee is examined by teams of law school professors as well as by a team of practicing lawyers.[169] The results of these various inquiries are then reported to the full 15-member Standing Committee for discussion and evaluation. At the completion of its review, the Standing Committee votes whether to rate the nominee "well qualified," "qualified," or "not qualified."[170]

In recent decades the typical practice of Presidents has been to choose their Supreme Court nominees quickly after a vacancy occurs on the Court, without receiving pre-nomination evaluation from the ABA Standing Committee.[171] While the practice serves to exclude the Standing Committee from the selection process, its evaluation nonetheless plays a prominent part later, in the Senate Judiciary Committee's consideration of the nomination. The Standing Committee's rating of a Supreme Court nominee received wide news coverage when it is sent to the Senate Judiciary Committee and when the chairmen of the Standing Committee appears before the Judiciary Committee, at the nominee's confirmation hearings, to explain the ABA committee's rating. After the hearings, it is a common practice for Members on the Judiciary Committee, and for other Senators, to cite the Standing Committee's rating of the nominee when explaining why they either support or oppose the nominee's confirmation.

Although well established, the standing Committee's involvement in the judicial nomination process in recent years has periodically been controversial. In

---

168 For example, when Robert H. Bork was nominated to the Supreme Court in 1987, the Standing Committee "interviewed Judge Bork, five members of the United States Supreme Court, many of his colleagues on the D.C. Circuit Court of Appeals, and approximately 170 federal and state court judges throughout the United States. The Committee also conducted interviews with approximately 150 practicing lawyers, 79 law school deans and professors, 11 of Judge Bork's former law clerks, and a number of attorneys who served under Bork when he was Solicitor General. The dean and 10 professors at the University of Michigan Law School examined Judge Bork's opinions for the Committee, which also received submissions from a number of institutions and groups." Ross, William G. Participation by the Public in the Federal Judicial Selection Process. *Vanderbilt Law Review,* v. 43, January 1990. p. 35, note 161. (Hereafter cited as Ross, Participation by the Public)

169 ABA, *Standing Committee,* pp. 8-9.

170 *Ibid.,* p. 9.

171 "Beginning with the nomination of William Brennan in 1956, the Justice Department... has notified the ABA of most prospective Supreme Court nominations twenty-four hours prior to their transmission to the Senate. " Ross, Participation by the Public, p. 38. Offered so shortly before the nomination, the Justice Department's notification serves essentially as a courtesy to the ABA rather than as an opportunity for the Standing Committee to assist or otherwise influence the President in deciding whom to nominate.

the mid-1980s, for example, political conservatives accused the Standing Committee of having a liberal bias against conservative judicial candidates. At one point, a politically conservative legal foundation assailed the Standing Committee for seeking input on prospective judicial nominees from more liberal interest groups, a practice that the Standing Committee subsequently discontinued.[172] In 1987, conservative groups again accused the Standing Committee of liberal bias after a minority of members on the committee rated Supreme Court nominee Robert H. Bork "not qualified" based in part on ideological considerations.[173] Subsequently, in 1989, the Standing Committee acceded to demands by the Bush Administration that thenceforth it leave out of its judicial evaluations any consideration of a nominee's political philosophy.[174]

Meanwhile, the Standing Committee also was under attack form the confidential manner in which it gathered its information and conducted its deliberations. Both conservative and liberal groups filed suits in highly publicized, but ultimately unsuccessful, efforts to enjoin the Justice Department from utilizing the evaluations of the Standing Committee until the latter made its meetings open to the public.[175] Similarly critical were various members of the Senate judiciary Committee, who contended that the ABA's Standing Committee had too influential a role in the judicial selection process.[176] In response to these

[172] The Washington Legal Foundation criticized this practice in conjunction with a lawsuit that it filed against the ABA Standing Committee, in which it alleged that the Committee's closed-door meetings were in violation of the Federal Advisory Committee Act's requirements that advisory committees to executive branch agencies conduct meetings open to the public. "The legal foundation's suit," one news story reported, "has forced a change at the ABA, which had been seeking comments on prospective nominees from such liberal groups as People for the American Way and the Alliance for Justice. After the Washington Legal Foundation demanded the candidates' names, the ABA committee said it would no longer share names with any outside groups." Kurtz, Howard. ABA Judge-Screening Panel Criticized. *Washington Post,* December 24. 1985. p. A13. See also Kamen, Al. Under Conservative Pressure, ABA Drops Judicial Panelist. *Washington Post,* July 18, 1986. p. A2; Biskupic, Joan. ABA's Role-Under Scrutiny in High Court, Senate. *Congressional Quarterly Weekly Report,* v. 47, April 22, 1989. p. 897. (Hereafter cited as Biskupic, ABA's Role Under Scrutiny)

[173] See: Thornton, Mary. The ABA's Judgments on Judges. *Washington Post,* September 25, 1987. p. A23; Kornhauser, Anne. ABA Dissenters Found Bork Too Rigid. *Legal Times*, v. 10, September 14. 1987. p. 15.

[174] See: Marcus, Ruth. ABA To Resume Role in Judicial Selection. *Washington Post,* June 3, 1989. p. A4; Ross, Participation by the Public, p. 36.

[175] The joint complaint of the Washington Legal Foundation and Public Citizen ultimately was disposed of by the Supreme Court in *Public Citizen v. United States Department of Justice,* 491 U.S. 440. (1989). In that decision the Court upheld a lower court's dismissal of the complaint, holding that the Federal Advisory Committee Act, which requires required Federal Advisory Committees to open their meetings, records and reports open to the public, does not apply to the ABA's Standing Committee on the Judiciary.

[176] Biskupic, ABA's Role Under Scrutiny, (see footnote 172) p. 896. Five Republican minority members of the Judiciary Committee maintained that the Standing Committee threatened to

and other criticisms, the Senate Judiciary Committee held a day-long hearing on June 1, 1989 on the ABA's role in evaluating judicial candidates.[177] While Senators used the event to "vent their dissatisfaction with the bar association," members of both parties also credited the ABA evaluation process with assisting Presidents "in choosing qualified candidates for the bench."[178]

In 1991 questions again were raised about the Standing Committee, this time over whether it was giving unduly favorable ratings to President Bush's judicial candidates. The issue arose in conjunction with the release of an academic study finding that President Bush's candidates for Federal judgeships had received higher marks from the ABA than those of the previous five Presidents. "Simmering behind the high ratings," the *Wall Street Journal* reported, was "a controversy over whether they were justified by the merit of the nominees or whether they were prompted by the ABA committee trying to preserve its role in the process."[179]

Most recently, in 1992, the ability of the ABA Standing Committee to conduct unbiased evaluations of judicial candidates came into question in yet another set of circumstances. The controversy was precipitated on August 11, 1992, when the ABA's House of Delegates, at its annual convention, voted 276 to 168 in favor of an abortion rights resolution, reversing a position of neutrality on the abortion question it had adopted in 1990.[180] The ABA action prompted 23

"eclipse the constitutional role" of the Judiciary Committee and the Senate as a whole; they urged the Senate to "de-institutionalize what is now a preeminent and quasi-public role" for the Standing Committee. *Ibid.*, p. 897. Likewise, a member of the Judiciary Committee's Democratic majority expressed concern that both the Administration and the Senate might be abdicating to the ABA some of their own responsibility in examining judicial nominees. "There are times," this Senator remarked, "when I hear senators say, "The ABA says he's OK, or he's not OK' – as if that's the whole issue." *Ibid.*, 897.

[177] U.S. Congress. Senate. Committee on the Judiciary. *The ABA Role in the Judicial Nomination Process.* Hearing on the Role of the American Bar Association in the Judicial Evaluation Process, 101st Cong., 1st Sess., June 2, 1989. Washington, U.S. Govt. Print. Off., 1991. 364p.

[178] Biskupic, Joan. Justice Department and ABA Settle their Differences. *Congressional Quarterly Weekly Report*, v. 47, June 3, 1989. p. 1327. "Democrats generally asked the ABA to scrutinize more carefully candidates' membership in clubs that exclude women and minorities and to weigh positively the legal work a candidate has done for the poor or needy. Republicans lashed out at [ABA officials appearing as witnesses before the Judiciary Committee] for activities those senators perceived as discriminating against conservatives. Committee Republicans, who had pushed for the hearing, also criticized the 'special relationship' the ABA has with the Justice Department." *Ibid.*

[179] Wermeil, Stelphen. Controversy Brews Behind High Marks Given to Bush Nominees for Judgeships. *Wall Street Journal,* May 13, 1991. p. B5. See also Arthurs, Rich. Reagan's Judges Rated a Bit Lower Than Carter's. *Legal Times,* v. 7, October 22, 1984. p. 16.

[180] See: Torry, Saundra. Lawyer's Group Votes To Back Abortion Rights. *Washington Post,* August 12, 1992; Samborn, Randall, and Victoria Slind-Flor. ABA '92: Feminism Is Theme. *National Law Journal,* v. 14, August 24, 1992. pp. 1, 34.

conservative organizations, in a letter to Attorney General William Barr, to demand that the Standing Committee be stripped of its role in evaluating judicial candidates. The organizations maintained that, in a political environment deeply divided on the abortion issue, a group must be neutral on abortion if it is to be allowed to evaluate prospective judges on behalf of the Government.[181] Disagreeing, the president of the ABA insisted that the Standing Committee would remain neutral when evaluating prospective judges, notwithstanding the bar association's stand on abortion.[182] Despite that assurance, Attorney General Barr said he was seriously considering downgrading or elimination the ABA's role in evaluating judicial candidates — because the ABA had taken stands, instead of remaining neutral, on a range of controversial issues including abortion.[183]

Subsequently, the debate over the Standing Committee's neutrality was put into sharper focus in two contrasting commentaries on the weekly publication *Legal Times*. In a September 14, 1992 commentary, Bruce Fein, a former associate deputy attorney general in the Reagan Administration, called for an end to the ABA's "charade of neutrality in rating nominees to the federal bench."[184] The ABA's passage of the resolution in favor of abortion rights, Mr. Fein maintained, "places the ABA at sharp odds with any judicial nominee suspected" of holding views opposed to those expounded in *Roe v. Wade,*[185] the landmark Supreme Court decision limiting the power of States to regulate abortion. The ABA, he contended, was also biased on other issues (citing, as examples, affirmative action, product liability, damage caps, the Legal Services Corporation, and access to the Federal courts) and frequently testified on legislation pending in Congress. "The ABA's unmistakable legal and political agenda," he concluded,

---

[181] The letter said that an end to the ABA's special advisory relationship with the Justice Department was called for, because by "its recent endorsement of the abortion agenda and other actions," the ABA had "chosen to be a political interest group rather than a non-political professional association." It noted that the ABA's incoming president planned to represent the ABA in lobbying for the Freedom of Choice Act, which would expand abortion rights. "Can anyone really believe," the letter asked, "that the ABA will implement its position by lobbying for federal legislation, but will suddenly refrain from implementing them in evaluating judicial candidates?" Roman, Nancy E. Conservatives: ABA Bias Taints Judge-Approval Role. *Washington Times,* August 14, 1992. p. A3.

[182] *Ibid.* See also McWilliams, J. Michael. Letters to the Editor: The ABA Has No Partisan Agenda. *Wall Street Journal,* November 25, 1992. p. 13.

[183] Roman, Nancy E. Judging of Judges May End. *Washington Times,* September 17, 1991. pp. A1, A8. Nonetheless, any inclination on Mr. Barr's part to stop receiving ABA evaluations on judicial candidates lost practical importance after election day, November 3, 1992. The election of Democratic Presidential candidate Bill Clinton meant that Attorney General Barr would be vacating his office prior to the resumption of the Judicial nomination process in 1993.

[184] Fein, Bruce. Let's Lower the ABA from Its Pedestal. *Legal Times,* v. 15, September 14, 1992. p. 28.

[185] 410 U.S. 113 (1973).

"discredits any claim to disinterest it could possibly have in rating judicial nominees."[186]

A rebuttal to Mr. Fein, appearing in the November 9, 1992 issue of *Legal Times,* was presented by Harold R. Tyler, Jr., a former U.S. district court judge, deputy attorney general in the Ford Administration, and chairman of the ABA Standing Committee from 1987 to 1989. Mr. Tyler noted that abortion was not the first controversial issue on which the ABA's delegates and officers had taken a position:

> This, not surprisingly, is a major reason why the ABA has taken steps to insulate the [Standing] committee from any suggestion of influence or bias. Although the committee is authorized to speak on behalf of the ABA, its ratings are not passed upon or "voted out" by the membership of the ABA. Indeed, it operates independently of the ABA Board of Governors and House of Delegates. Only committee members are involved in its processes; committee records and information are confidential; and neither ABA officers nor any other ABA committee exercises any influence or control over reports by the committee to the executive or legislative branches of government.[187]

The Standing Committee's procedures, Mr. Tyler concluded, are "carefully structured to achieve an impartial evaluation of a candidate's professional qualifications based upon the reports of the candidate's peers." He expressed his conviction that the Standing Committee performs "a most useful role on helping promote a more qualified and able federal judiciary… ."[188]

In the summer of the 1992 the issue of the ABA's neutrality was argued primarily in the context of rating candidates for lower court judgeships on behalf of the Justice Department. However, the neutrality of the ABA's Standing Committee in the future might also loom as a reform issue in the Senate, in the context of Supreme Court nominations. This might happen if positions taken by the ABA on controversial issues are regarded as biasing the Standing Committee in assessing the qualifications of Supreme Court nominees. Because of the

---

[186] Fein, Let's Lower the ABA, p. 28.

[187] Tyler, Harold R., Jr. In Defense of the ABA's Role in Rating Nominees. *Legal Times,* v. 15, November 9, 1992. p. 37.
See also McWilliams, J. Michael. Letters to the Editor: The ABA Has No Partisan Agenda. *Wall Street Journal,* November 25, 1992. p. A13, in which Mr. McWilliams, the president of the ABA, States: "While the ABA has adopted hundreds of policy positions on legislative issues, none of these ever been or will ever be a factor in the Standing Committee's evaluation of prospective candidate. …There is no 'litmus test' and the committee has never asked prospective nominees for their views on ABA policy positions."

[188] *Ibid.*

importance typically attached to a Supreme Court nominee's ABA rating, Members of the Senate can be expected to be sensitive to any questions concerning the Standing Committee's neutrality in exercising its evaluating role.

Role of Partisan Interest Groups Which Support or Oppose a Nominee

Another question which has arisen is whether reform should extend to the role of partisan interest groups that actively support or oppose a Supreme Court nominee. Such groups became a focal point for criticism from various quarters during and immediately after the Senate's consideration of the nomination of Clarence Thomas to the Court.

One criticism was that some interest groups resorted to unscrupulous practices in order to discredit the nominee or other persons who were playing prominent roles on the confirmation process. For instance, Senator John C. Danforth of Missouri, a prominent supporter of the nominee, faulted interest groups opposed to Judge Thomas for allegedly "pawing through every statement that he made" in order to find something unfavorable about him.[189] President Bush expressed a similar sentiment. The Thomas hearings, according to the President, "sent our people this kind of false message: If you want to make a difference, don't enter public service. Join a special interest group, whether it's the right or the left, and that way you can fight as hard as you want, or as dirty as you want, without any responsibility for the results."[190]

Another criticism was that interest groups tended to distort the political process, by mobilizing their supporters to apply intense pressures upon the Senate during its consideration of the Thomas nomination. President Bush said that at the Judiciary Committee hearings on the Thomas nomination, the public "saw outside pressure groups exhorting and twisting. ..."[191] As the Senate moved to postpone its vote on the Thomas nomination for a week, to allow for new committee hearings into allegations of misconduct made against Judge Tomas, Senator

---

[189] Danforth, John C. Supreme Court of the United States. Remarks in the Senate. *Congressional Record,* Daily Edition, October 3, 1991. p. S14283.

[190] Bush, Remarks to Public Administration Groups (see footnote 63), p. 1496. Earlier in his remarks the President was even more critical of outside interest groups: "Some people have tried to drag public debate to a new low, searching openly for dirt – any dirt – without regard to people's rights to privacy, sometimes without concern for the facts. While crusading pressure groups talk about their favorite issues, they forget that human beings sit there beneath the glare of the spotlight, vulnerable to assaults from all quarters. The piranha tactics of smearing the individual and ignoring the issue serve no public purpose. They aim to destroy lives and wreck reputations." *Ibid.*

[191] *Ibid.*

Danforth predicted ruefully that "It is going to be a field day for all the groups ginning up all the phone calls and all the pressure on Senators."[192]

Members of the Judiciary Committee also have expressed concerns about the influence of interest groups on the confirmation process. Senator Dennis DeConcini, for example, has remarked:

> I cannot deny that the techniques of grass roots lobbying have become more sophisticated and effective over the years. Unfortunately, special interest groups usually evaluate a nominee upon the basis of a single issue. I believe this distorts the process. The choice of a Supreme Court Justice should not be a referendum on the hottest issue of the day.[193]

In the view of another Judiciary Committee member, Senator Charles E. Grassley of Iowa, special interest groups during the Thomas confirmation battle functioned as a "shadow Senate." In that role, he has maintained, they exercised advice and consent functions that the Constitution reserves for the Senate:

> They conducted a large part of the investigation that normally would be done by congressional investigators. These non-Government investigators, not publicly responsible to the people by the way, decided what information would come out about the nominee, when that would happen, and even where it would happen.[194]

Senator Grassley expressed his hope for a "return to a process in which advocacy groups are not the key players" in determining whether a Supreme Court nominee is confirmed.[195]

One suggested reform would make the role played by interest groups in the Supreme Court confirmation process more subject to Senate and public scrutiny. Such an approach has been advocated by Representative E. Thomas Coleman (R-MO). In his view, the "sorry spectacle" of the Thomas confirmation process was in large part "the product of relentless and ruthless campaigns by well-heeled special interest groups whose activities were hidden by current law, which casts a legal veil over their activities." As a corrective measure, Representative Coleman introduced H.R. 3226, which would require all individuals and organizations spending money to support or oppose a Supreme Court nominee to file Federal

[192] Danforth, John C. Unanimous Consent Agreement. Remarks in the Senate. *Congressional Record,* Daily Edition, v. 137, October 8, 1991. p. S14569.

[193] DeConcini, Examining the Process (see footnote 27), p. 21.

[194] Grassley, Charles E. The Nomination Process. Remarks in the Senate. *Congressional Record,* Daily Edition, v. 138, July 2, 1992. p. S9574.

[195] *Ibid.*

disclosure forms similar to those required of congressional and Presidential campaigns. In the process, according to Representative Coleman, the bill would help Senators know "who is contributing to and staging these campaigns for or against Supreme Court nominees."[196] The bill, however, received no House action before the final adjournment of the 102d Congress in October 1992.

Any reform measure to restrict the public participation of interest groups in the confirmation process might be expected to generate some opposition. It would seem inherently controversial by virtue of running counter to the trend in recent years in which the Senate has allowed an increasing number of interest group spokespersons and other witnesses to testify at Supreme Court confirmation hearings.[197] Senator DeConcini, a member of the Judiciary Committee, has commented that he would not support "a curtailment of the access special interest groups have to the Committee," notwithstanding what he saw as their tendency to "distort the process." These groups, he noted, "often have large constituencies, representing proponents and opponents. They have a right to voice their opinions on a decision that will have a tremendous impact on their lives."[198]

Instead, Senator DeConcini has suggested, one "possible reform" would be "to allow the nominee to respond to groups who testify after his or her initial testimony." The Senator explained why he looked favorably on this option:

> Under the current format, the nominee appears for committee questioning, followed by individuals and representatives of groups testifying in support

---

[196] Coleman, E, Thomas. Reform the Supreme Court Confirmation Process. Remarks in the House. *Congressional Record,* Daily Edition, v. 137, October 16, 1991. pp. H7870-71.

[197] Prior to the Souter and Thomas confirmation processes in 1990 and 1991 respectively, one legal scholar wrote: "The sharp contrast between the public controversy over the recent Rehnquist and Bork nominations and the widespread public silence concerning the Scalia and Kennedy nominations suggest that organized interest groups are not likely to have a significant role in every nomination. A clear trend, however exists, toward an increased public awareness of the importance of federal judicial nominations and a growing public participation in the selection process." Ross, William G. Participation by the Public in the Federal Judicial Selection Process. *Vanderbilt Law Review,* v. 43, January 1990. p. 1. Ross's article concerned the influence of interest groups not only on the selection of judicial nominees on the pre-hearing stage, but also on the over-all confirmation process (including hearings, Senate committee action, and Senate floor debate).

[198] DeConcini, Examining the Process, p. 21. See also Ross, Participation by the Public, p. 26, in which the author contends: "Although there are good reasons for retaining an appointive judiciary, the exclusion of public participation in a process that has so vast an impact upon the lives of virtually all American would contravene the democratic character of American government. Accordingly, individuals and special interest groups should be encouraged to make their views known to the President prior to the nomination and to the Senate during the confirmation process. A robust participation by the public in the prenomination and confirmation processes assures that the judicial selection process will take proper account of the public will."

> for or opposition to the nominee. This format permits the nominee's opponents to scrutinize the nominee's testimony for inconsistencies, contradictions or other faults. The nominee should, at a minimum, be offered the opportunity to respond to opposition testimony.[199]

A different kind of approach to the interest group question has been proposed by the chairman of the Judiciary Committee, Senator Biden. The has suggested that, to prevent interest groups in the future from "defining the debate and dictating the tactics," Senators should begin public discussion on a Supreme Court nomination well before confirmation hearings begin.[200] In the past, he said, when Senators have announced their opposition to a Supreme Court nominee prior to the confirmation hearings, they often have been faulted by the news media for prejudging the nominee's fitness. Yet, in Chairman Biden's view, Senators who refrain from publicly taking stands on, expressing their concerns about, a nominee until the start of hearings create an unfortunate "vacuum," which in turn is quickly filled by interest groups:

> The criticism of taking early stands on nominees has pushed Senators out of the summer debate over confirmation and left that debate to others, most especially the interest groups on the left and the right. Instead of respected Senators on the left and right, arguing prior to the hearing about the philosophy of the nominee, when we stood back, that vacuum was filled... by the left and the right as is their right, I might add. But they are the only voices that we heard in the debate."[201]

In the future, Senator Biden maintained, the onus is on Members of the Senate to move the focus "from the tactics of the confirmation debate to the substance of it... ." Before the start of confirmation hearings he urged his colleagues, "begin the debate in the issues because, when we do not, we have learned [in] this town, the press, interest groups and political parties fill the vacuum."[202]

---

[199] *Ibid.*
[200] Biden, Reform of Confirmation Process (see footnote 18), p. S8864.
[201] *Ibid.*
[202] *Ibid.*

Senate's Decision Whether to Confirm or Reject

Debate over proposed reform of the Supreme Court appointment process also has focused on the process by which the Senate as a whole decides whether to confirm or reject the President's nominee. Recent discussions have most frequently touched on one aspect of this process — the criteria used by the Senate in evaluating a Supreme Court nomination. Another, much less publicized subject for proposed reform has been the kind of Senate majority that should be required for confirmation.

Criteria Used by Senate

Shortly after the Senate voted on October 15, 1991 to confirm the Supreme Court nomination of Clarence Thomas, a legal scholar wrote that the Thomas confirmation battle "revives a broad issue." The issue, he stated, was "how active the Senate should be in rejecting a nominee on ideological grounds."[203] During the Thomas confirmation process, the nominee's judicial philosophy or "ideology" assumed a prominence that was reminiscent of its central place in the Senate's contentious debate over Supreme Court nominee Robert H. Bork in 1987. Essentially the issue both in 1987 and 1991 was whether the Senate, in evaluating a Supreme Court nominee, should weigh other considerations besides his or her professional qualifications and character.

Prior to the Bork nomination, the Senate, according to one commentator, had been inclined to give the President "his pick once you satisfy considerations of ability, integrity and competence."[204] During the Bork confirmation process, however, another school of thought emerged in the Senate which was less deferential to the President. The Senate, some now argued, should perform a more independent and questioning function. Rather than defer to the President, and accept his nominee if the latter met the standard criteria of ability, integrity and temperament, the Senate might also, according to this school of thought, appropriately consider the nominee's judicial philosophy, ideological or political orientation, and positions on specific legal controversies.[205]

---

203 Friedman, Richard D. Senate Should Use the Option of Closed Hearing. *Christian Science Monitor,* October 24, 1991. p. 17. The author is identified as a professor of law at the University of Michigan Law School.

204 University of Michigan law professor Yale Kamisar, quoted in Kamen, Al, and Ruth Marcus. Nomination to Test Senate Role in Shaping of Supreme Court; Democratic Senators Taking More Aggressive Stance This Year. *Washington Post,* July 1. 1987. p. A9.

205 See, for example, U.S. Library of Congress. Congressional Research Service. *Senate Consideration of the Nomination of Robert H. Bork To Be a Supreme Court Associate Justice:*

The argument that the Senate should use ideological or political considerations in evaluating Supreme Court nominees was spurred in large part by the unique circumstances of the Bork nomination. President Ronald Reagan had explicitly cited philosophical reasons for his nominating Judge Bork.[206] Outside the White House the Bork nomination was viewed as of historic importance, and highly controversial, in light of the change it might bring to the Court. The nomination of Judge Bork, the *New York Times* reported, was "widely seen as tipping the ideological balance of the Court to the right."[207] The nomination prompted immediate reactions from conservative groups fervently in favor of his confirmation and from liberal organizations as fervently opposed.[208]

The ideological implications of the Bork nomination were cited at the time by various Senate Members who favored a relatively broad scope of inquiry extending well beyond the nominee's legal skills and character. Among these Members was Chairman Biden. In "recent times, under normal circumstances," he noted, when the Senate has considered a Supreme Court nomination, many Senators have preferred "not to consider questions of judicial philosophy," restricting their assessment of the nominee "to questions of character and of competence." They have applied this relatively narrow standard, Mr. Biden asserted, when the President has selected nominees "on the basis of their detachment and their statesmanship."[209] However, senator Biden continued, when a President selects a nominee on the basis of judicial philosophy, the Senate in turn has the right to widen the scope of its inquiry to include the nominee's judicial philosophy and the consequences for the country of his or her nomination.[210] As to the Bork nomination, Senator Biden maintained, the Senate had both the right and the duty to raise political and judicial "questions of

Background and an Overview of Issues. Report No. 87-761 GOV, by Denis Steven Rutkus. Washington, D.C., 1987. pp. 19-25. (Hereafter cited as Rutkus, *Senate Consideration of Bork Nomination)*

206 "Judge Bork, widely regarded as the most prominent and intellectually powerful advocate of judicial restraint, shares my views that judges' personal preferences and values should not be part of their constitutional interpretations. The guiding principle of judicial restraint recognizes that under Constitution it is the exclusive province of the legislatures to enact laws and the role of the courts to interpret them." U.S. President, 1981-89 (Reagan). Supreme Court of the United States; Remarks Announcing the Nomination of Robert H. Bork To Be An Associate Justice, July 1, 1987. *Weekly Compilation of Presidential Documents,* v. 23, July, 6, 1987. p. 761.

207 Boyd, Gerald M. Bork Picked for High Court; Reagan cites His 'Restraint;' Confirmation Fight Looms. *New York Times,* July 2, 1987. p. A1.

208 Rutkus, Senate Consideration of Bork Nomination, p. 10.

209 Biden, Joseph R., Jr. Advice and Consent: The Right and Duty of the Senate To Protect the Integrity of the Supreme Court. Remarks in the Senate. *Congressional Record,* Daily Edition, v. 133, July 23, 1987. p. S10527.

210 *Ibid.*, p. S10527-28.

substance," for "we are once again confronted with a popular President's determined attempt to bend the Supreme Court to his political ends."[211]

By contrast, other Senate Members, most of whom favored the nominee's confirmation, expressed a preference for a narrower scope of Senate inquiry focusing on Judge Bork's legal competence and character. They asserted that the nominee's political and social views were largely or totally irrelevant to the question of his fitness to serve on the Court. Still others considered Judge Bork's judicial philosophy and views of the Senate to make in these areas, it was argued, was whether his views fell within a broad range of acceptable thinking, not whether individual Senators agreed with those views. Further, some Senators argued, to evaluate a nominee according to political or judicial philosophy, or to vote to confirm only if Senators agreed with the nominee's views, would politicize the Supreme Court and undermine its independence of the legislative branch.[212]

In common with the Bork nomination, President George Bush's nomination of Clarence Thomas to the Supreme Court in July 1991 was controversial from the outset. Prior to his appointment in 1989 to the U.S. Circuit Court of Appeals for the District of Columbia, Judge Thomas had served in high-visibility posts for eight years in the Reagan Administration. There he had gained a reputation as a political conservative who was outspokenly critical of affirmative action as an approach to promoting equal opportunity under the law. Liberals in the Senate feared, among other things, that past Supreme Court decisions upholding abortion rights and affirmative action laws would be jeopardized by Judge Thomas's appointment to the Court.[213]

As with the Bork nomination, disagreements again arose within the Senate on the criteria to use in evaluating Judge Thomas's fitness to serve on the Court. Some Senators focused largely or exclusively on the nominee's professional qualifications. In this vein, a Senator declared that instead of considering Judge Thomas' "philosophy on particular issues" which might come before the Supreme Court, the "more appropriate standard" for reviewing the nominee's qualifications was the standard articulated by the American Bar Association in determining that

---

[211] *Ibid.*, p. S10529.

[212] Rutkus, Senate Consideration of Bork Nomination, pp. 25-27.

[213] See, for example: Biskupic, Joan. Democrats To Push Thomas on Abortion, Other Views. *Congressional Quarterly Weekly Report,* v. 49, July 6, 1991. p. 1826-28; Bedard, Paul. Young Conservative Stirs Liberal Tempers. *Washington Times,* July 2, 1991. pp. A1, A6; Garrett, Major. Grilling on Hill Awaits Nominee. *Washington Times,* July 2, 1991. pp.A1, A6; Marcus, Ruth. Thomas Seen Facing Abortion Questions. *Washington Post,* July 4, 1991. p. A12.

a candidate was "qualified."[214] The ABA, the Senator noted, required "that the nominee 'have outstanding legal ability and a wide experience and meet the highest standards of integrity, judicial temperament, and professional competence.'" Another Senator remarked that it was "a fundamental misunderstanding of the Senate's role in the confirmation process for Senators to vote against nominees "unless they hold views consistent with our own."[215] The time of Senators, he continued,

> would be much better spent looking at the personal side of the nominee. We would focus on the family background, personal character, intellectual independence of the nominee. We should focus on his moral Constitution and his value system.[216]

However, in assessing Judge Thomas's fitness to serve on the Court, other Senators ascribed a higher priority to the nominee's judicial philosophy or views on particular constitutional issues. One Senator, for example maintained that if Members of the Senate were "not confident that nominees possess a clear commitment to the fundamental constitutional rights and freedoms at the heart of our democracy, they should not be confirmed."[217] Another Senator told his Senate colleagues that he was using the "same criteria" to evaluate Judge Thomas as he had in 1990 when examining the qualifications of Supreme Court nominee David H. Souter. "I was then, as I am now," the Senator stated, "most concerned about preserving individual civil liberties."[218] A third Senator maintained that it was appropriate under the circumstances of the Thomas nomination for the Senate to take the nominee's "ideology" into account:

> When the president makes the political decision to tip the balance of the Court and pack it with people having a rightwing ideology, then the Senate has the right to do the people's business and reject those nominees.[219]

---

[214] Murkowski, Frank H. Nomination of Clarence Thomas to the Supreme Court. Remarks in the Senate. *Congressional Record,* Daily Edition, v. 137, October 1, 1991. p. S14037.

[215] Hatfield, Mark O. Nomination of Clarence Thomas, of Georgia, To Be an Associate Justice of the Supreme Court of the United States. Remarks in the Senate. *Congressional Record,* Daily Edition, v. 137, October 3, 1991. S14322.

[216] *Ibid.,* p. S14323.

[217] Kennedy, Edward M. Supreme Court on the United States. Remarks in the Senate. *Congressional Record,* v. 137, October 3, 1991. p. S14298.

[218] Akaka, Daniel K. Supreme Court of the United States. Remarks in the Senate. *Congressional Record,* Daily Edition, v. 137, October 3, 1991. p. S14304.

[219] Leahy, Patrick J. Advice and Consent. Remarks in the Senate. *Congressional Record,* Daily Edition, v. 137, October 24, 1991. p. S15117.

During Senate debate over the Thomas nomination, the range of differing viewpoints over the issue of judicial philosophy was noted by Senator Strom Thurmond, the ranking Republican on the Senate Judiciary Committee. "Some argue," Senator Thurmond noted, "that philosophy should not be considered at all in the nomination process, while others state that philosophy should be the sole criteria." In Senator Thurmond's view, it was inappropriate "that philosophy alone should bar a nominee from the Supreme Court unless that nominee holds a belief that is contrary to the fundamental, longstanding principles of our Nation." To require a nominee to pass a philosophical or controversial topics "litmus test," Senator Thurmond contended, would "seriously jeopardize" the Federal judiciary's independence.[220]

Some months after the Thomas vote, chairman Biden offered the view that the senate had been compelled by the Bork and Thomas nominations to make the judicial philosophy of each nominee a major consideration. Through these nominations, Senator Biden asserted, Presidents Reagan and Bush "attempted to move the Court ideologically into a radical, new direction which this country does not support," posing an "unprecedented challenge" to the Supreme Court confirmation process. In response, according to Senator Biden:

> ...we in the Senate developed an unprecedented confirmation process. The centerpiece of this new process was a frank recognition of the legitimacy of Senate consideration of a nominee's judicial philosophy as part of the confirmation review.[221] (Emphasis added)

Recent debate over the Supreme Court confirmation process has served again to bring into the public spotlight the question of which criteria are most valid for the Senate to use in evaluating a nominee. As the preceding paragraphs indicate, some Senators have cited a nominee's professional qualifications, others have stressed the importance of the nominee's judicial philosophy or views on constitutional issues, while still others have indicated that they have been influenced in varying degrees by both kind of criteria. The actual criteria used in

---

220 Thurmond, Strom. Supreme Court of the United States. Remarks in the Senate. *Congressional Record,* Daily Edition, v. 137, October 3, 1991. p. S14285.

221 Biden, Reform of Confirmation Process (see footnote 18), p. S8854. Senator Biden made these observations in extended Senate floor remarks eight months after the Senate's vote to confirm Clarence Thomas to the Court. "In my view," he stated later in his remarks, "the debate over the Senate's review of ideology has been fruitful. We have quashed the myth that the Senate must defer to a President's choice of a Supreme court Justice, the men and women at the apex of the independent third branch of Government. As the Senate properly does for nominees in the executive branch, the role of the Senate as a vital partner in reviewing Supreme Court nominations has been enhanced." *Ibid.,* p. 8860.

evaluating a Supreme Court nominee typically have been a personal, very individual matter for each Senator.

The Kind of Majority Required for Confirmation

Another reform question raised in connection with the Supreme Court appointments process has been whether Senate confirmation should require the affirmative vote of more than a simple majority of its Members.

Since the time of George Washington's Presidency to the present day period, the Senate, whenever it has approved a Supreme Court nomination, has done so by a simple majority of its Members present and voting. The relevant part of the Constitution, Article II, Section 2, does not specify the kind of Senate majority which is needed. It merely provides that the President "shall nominate, and by and with the Advice and Consent of the Senate, shall appoint... Judges of the Supreme Court." However, the immediately preceding sentence in Article II, Section 2 explicitly stipulates that the President shall have the power to make *treaties* "provided two-thirds of the Senators present concur." Given the express two thirds requirement for treaty ratification, one scholar has observed, "it is a reasonable inference that judicial confirmations were intended to be by a bare majority."[222]

A higher voting majority requirement, under which nominations to the Court would be confirmed only upon the approval of two thirds of Senators present and voting, has been proposed by the scholar quoted above. The history of Supreme Court nominations, he notes, has been "replete with controversy, acrimony, and partisan politics," with approximately one of every five nominations having failed.[223] At the core of such controversy between the President and the Senate, he maintains, have been "poor appointments" that failed to show "[m]utual respect and a decent regard for governmental institutions... ."[224]

A requirement of a two thirds affirmative vote of the Senate for confirmation would be designed to address this problem. According to its advocate, the two

---

[222] Massey, Calvin R. Getting There: A Brief History of the Politics of Supreme Court Appointments. *Hastings Constitutional Law Quarterly,* v. 19, Fall 1991. p. 14. (Hereafter cited as Massey, Getting There) The author is identified in an introductory note as Professor of Constitutional Law, University of California, Hastings College of the Law. *Ibid.*, p. 1.

[223] *Ibid.*, p. 1.

[224] *Ibid.*, pp. 13-14. "Andrew Jackson, for example, believed that the best way to deal with senatorial rejection of a Presidential nominee was wither to leave the post vacant or to offer another nominee even less palatable than the first. Jackson's appointments to the Court were hardly stellar. [Richard] Nixon's attempt to emulate Jackson's strategy produced[Supreme Court nominee] Harrold Carswell. Mutual respect and a decent regard for governmental institutions would decrease the likelihood that pique will produce judicial disasters." *Ibid.*

thirds rule would encourage a President to choose from among the most distinguished persons available and compel him "to select a nominee with broad public support."[225] The scholar cautions that the thrust of his suggestion "is not to claim it will produce better justices in every instance if its application, but to suggest that the addition of another structural check might lessen the institutional costs that the current process seems to impose."[226]

Published after the Senate in October 1991 confirmed the Clarence Thomas nomination, the proposal to require a two thirds vote to confirm future Supreme nominations appears so far to have escaped the Senate's attention in its public discussions of possible reforms. In the absence thus far of debate on the proposal's merits, the scholar himself has volunteered several possible criticisms that could be made.[227]

First, he has predicted, a two thirds rule "would inevitably increase the impact of special interest groups because they would be able to block any nomination if they could garner the support of one-third of the Senate's members plus one." While this might "appear to be a defect," it is one that could "be readily overcome." He explained:

> A premium would be placed on nominating a person whose accomplishments, constitutional philosophy, and professional stature are so beyond cavil that even groups politically opposed to the nominee would fail to arouse senatorial opposition. Not every Justice will be a Benjamin Cardozo, but the possible of special interest checks will increase the odds that a larger proportion of nominees will look more like Cardozo than [Clarence] Thomas.[228]

A second possible adverse effect of a two thirds rule would be to "produce an utterly colorless nominee, without any track record." To "avoid triggering opposition from interest groups," the President might be "tempted to send up a nominee lacking any background"[229] Yet, it can also be argued, a two thirds rule might actually *discourage* such selections as a President would know that his nomination would be in jeopardy if only one third of the Senate's Members were offended by the nominee's lack of distinction.

---

[225] *Ibid.*, p. 15.

[226] *Ibid.*, p. 16.

[227] Research by CRS located no articles taking issue with Professor Massey's proposal, and in a telephone interview with CRS on December 23, 1992 he said he was unaware of any published rebuttals to his law journal article.

[228] Massey, Getting There, p. 15.

[229] Massey, Calvin R. Professor of Constitutional Law, University of California, Hastings college of the Law. Telephone interview, December 23, 1992.

A third objection which might be raised to this proposed reform is the possibility that it would require amending the Constitution. The process of amending the Constitution, provided for in Article V, is protracted and difficult. A proposed amendment first requires approval either of a two thirds majority vote in both the House and the Senate or of a convention called by Congress on the application of the legislatures of two thirds of the States. The amendment then must be ratified by the legislatures or *ad hoc* conventions in three quarters of the States. Members of the Senate (and of the House as well) might regard skeptically any reform of the confirmation process that would entail amending the Constitution; they might be expected to question whether the reform would be of sufficient merit to justify the considerable commitment of time and energy involved in securing its adoption.

Mindful of this likely objection, the scholar in favor of a two thirds "supermajority" for confirmation to the Supreme Court has suggested that the reform might be accomplished by means other than constitutional amendment. It could plausibly be argued, he maintains, that Congress has the power to effect the reform by ordinary legislation:

> ...since the judicial confirmation clause [in the Constitution] does not expressly declare that the consent required is by a simple majority, it is at least arguable that the majority necessary for exercise of the consent power bestowed on the Senate may be altered from time to time by ordinary legislation. In any event, were Congress to enact legislation creating a two-thirds consent requirement, it s possible that the validity of that action would be a nonjusticiable political question.[230]

Overall Length of Process

Another issue concerning the Supreme Court appointment process has been whether the overall process has become too drawn out, and if so what should be done to shorten it. Members in the Senate have disagreed on whether 100 days, for instance, is too long a duration for a Supreme Court nomination to be pending in the Senate. Critics have argued that such an extent of time is too long for a nominee to be exposed to personal attacks by opponents, causes the confirmation

---

[230] Massey, Getting There, p. 14. In a footnote (*Ibid.*, note 43) the author for support cited *Goldwater v. Carter,* 444 U. S. 996 (1979), finding the power of the President unilaterally to abrogate a treaty to be nonjusticiable, and *Coleman v. Miller,* 307 U.S. 433 (1939), holding the efficacy of the purported state ratification of a constitutional amendment to be a nonjusticiable political question.

process to become overly contentious, and may prevent a nominee, if eventually confirmed, from being appointed on time to start work with the other Justices on the Court when it starts its annual term in October. Others, however, have defended an extended confirmation process, even one running as long as 100 days. The uniquely important nature of a Supreme Court appointment, it has been argued, obligates the Senate to be especially deliberate and painstaking in considering the qualifications and suitability of nominee for membership on the Nation's highest court.

During the Reagan and Bush Presidencies it became routine, after the President submitted a Supreme Court nomination, for two to three months to elapse before the Senate took final action on the nomination. Although President Reagan's first Supreme Court appointee, Sandra Day O'Connor, was confirmed in 1981 only 33 days after being nominated, the overall process for each Reagan and Bush nomination thereafter became much more protracted: 89 days for William H. Rehnquist in 1986 (to be Chief Justice); 85 days for Antonin Scalia in 1986; 108 days for Robert H. Bork in 1987; 65 days for Anthony M. Kennedy in 1987-88; 69 days for David H. Souter in 1990; and 99 days for Clarence Thomas in 1991.

These time spans represented a significant expansion of time devoted to the appointment process over what the Senate historically had afforded to Supreme Court nominations. From the Presidencies of George Washington (1789-97) to William Howard Taft (1909-13) the Senate took final action on the vast majority of Supreme Court nominations within a week of receiving a nomination from the President.[231] From the Presidencies of Woodrow Wilson (1913-21) to John F. Kennedy (1961-63), the overall confirmation process for the vast majority of nominations fell into the one to four-week range, and President Lyndon Johnson's first Supreme Court nomination, of Abe Fortas in 1965 to be an Associate Justice, was processed in 14 days. [232] However, from that point onward, to the present day, the Supreme Court appointment process more often than not was significantly longer than it ordinarily had been for persons nominated during the decades spanning the Wilson and Kennedy Presidencies.[233] From President Johnson's nomination of Thurgood Marshall in 1967 through George Bush's nomination of Clarence Thomas on 1991, 11 out of 17 Supreme Court nominations were under

[231] See table of nomination and confirmation dates for Supreme Court nominations from 1789 to 1989 in Witt, Elder. *Congressional Quarterly's Guide to the U.S. Supreme Court,* 2d Ed. Washington, D.C., Congressional Quarterly Inc., 1990. pp. 995-98.

[232] *Ibid.*

[233] See U.S. Library of Congress. Congressional Research Service. *The Speed with Which Action Has Been Taken on Supreme Court Nominations in the Last 25 Years.* Report 87-576 GOV, by Denis Steven Rutkus. Washington, D.C., 1897. 15 p.

Senate consideration for more than nine weeks;[234] more than eleven weeks elapsed, following the President's nomination action, before 8 of the 11 nominations received final Senate action.[235] A few of the nominations between the Johnson and Reagan Presidencies, it should be acknowledged, were processed with a speed characteristic of the earlier historical periods.[236] Also, the Senate's extended deliberations over the Bork and Thomas nominations in 1987 and 1991 respectively were not without historical precedents.[237] However, not until the Reagan and Bush Presidencies had six consecutive Supreme Court nominees been considered by the Senate for such extended periods as noted in the preceding paragraph.

Various factors have played a part in causing the Senate in the last two decades to take more time in acting on Supreme Court nominations than it has previously. First, in the 1970s, as one scholar has observed, "the Senate began to intensify its scrutiny of presidential nomination."[238] As part of this trend, the Senate Judiciary Committee, by the end of the decade, had created its own investigative staff unit,[239] which it continued to augment in the 1980s.[240] This

---

[234] Of the eleven nominations, six were confirmed by the Senate – those of Marshall in 1967, Rehnquist and Scalia in 1986, Kennedy in 1988, Souter in 1990, and Thomas in 1991; three were rejected outright by the Senate – those of Clement Haynsworth in 1969, G. Harrold Carswell in 1970, and Robert H. Bork in 1987; another, that of Abe Fortas in 1986 (to be Chief Justice), was in effect rejected by the Senate when a motion to close debate on the nomination failed; and one, that of Homer Thornberry 1968 (to fill the Associate Justice vacancy that would have been created on the Court if Justice Fortas had been confirmed to be Chief Justice), was withdrawn from the Senate by President Johnson without ever having been reported out of Committee.

[235] The nominations and times which elapsed were: Marshall in 1967, 78 days; Fortas in 1968, 97 days; Clement Haynsworth in 1969, 92 days; G. Harrold Carswell in 1970, 79 days; Rehnquist and Scalia in 1986, 89 and 85 days respectively, Bork in 1987, 108 days; and Thomas in 1991, 99 days.

[236] After being nominated, two of President Richard Nixon's appointees, Warren E. Burger (in 1969) and Henry A. Blackmun (in 1970), respectively were confirmed by the Senate 17 and 27 days later. In 1975 President Gerald R. Ford's only Supreme Court appointee, John Paul Stevens, was confirmed by the Senate 16 days after being nominated.

[237] Earlier in American history, two other Supreme Court nominations were pending in the Senate for longer periods of time than the Bork and Thomas nominations. On January 15, 1894, the senate by a 30-24 vote rejected the Supreme Court nomination of William B. Hornblower 118 days after receiving it from President Grover Cleveland. On June 1, 1916, the Senate by a 47-22 vote confirmed the nomination of Louis D. Brandeis 125 days after receiving it from President Woodrow Wilson. See table of nomination and confirmation dates for Supreme Court nominations from 1789 to 1989 in Witt, Elder. *Congressional Quarterly's Guide to the U.S. Supreme Court,* 2d Ed. Washington, D.C., Congressional Quarterly Inc., 1990. pp. 995-98.

[238] Markenzie, G. Calvin. *The Politics of Presidential Appointments.* New York, The Free Press. 1981. p. 105.

[239] With the passage of the Omnibus Judgeship Act in October 1987, "both the administration and Congress went on record in support of merit selection [of judges]. The committee significantly

allowed the Committee to conduct its own intensive investigations of judicial appointees, including Supreme Court nominees, and to be less dependent on the background investigations of the executive branch's Federal Bureau of Investigation.[241] A bona fide staff background investigation by specially trained Committee staff necessarily meant that at least few additional weeks would be injected into the prehearing phase of each Supreme Court nomination, and possibly more time as well if staff investigations uncovered now leads that needed to be pursued.

A second factor causing the confirmation process of many recent Supreme Court nominations to be drawn out would be their controversial nature. The Supreme Court nominations of Abe Fortas (1968, to be Chief Justice), Clement Haynsworth (1969), G. Harrold Carswell (1970), William H. Renhquist (1971, and again in 1986, to be Chief Justice), Robert H. Bork (1987) and Clarence Thomas (1991), all generated considerable controversy in the Senate. For each nomination, there were several days of hearings, more than one day of Senate debate, and a sizable Senate vote cast against confirmation (or against closing Senate debate on the nomination). In each instance the nomination process became embroiled in highly sensitive police questions concerning the role and future direction of the Supreme Court, and in debate over what confirmation of the nominee might mean for the Nation's welfare. Also contributing to the sense of controversy over each of these nominations were partisan tensions between the political parties, with Senate Members of the President's party usually supporting the nomination, and most of the Senate opposition to a nomination coming from the other party in the Senate. Such circumstances worked against any efforts to secure prompt Committee or Senate action on the nominations in question.

Third, since the 1980s the creation of each new Supreme Court vacancy has occurred at a time of year that was convenient for extended hearings preparation by the Senate Judiciary Committee. Each annual term of the Supreme Court

---

expanded its investigative role in the confirmation process as it established a thorough procedure for reviewing the qualifications of those candidates nominated by the President. "The committee has employed an investigative staff, responsible for careful study and analysis of the Background and qualifications on nominees, including access to FBI files." U.S. Congress. Senate. Committee on the Judiciary. *Annual Activities Report.* Committee Print, 96th Cong., 2d Sess. Washington, U.S. Govt. Print. off., 1980. p. 70.

[240] See Moran, Terence. Battle over Judges Brews in the Senate, Democrats Beef Up Investigations with More Staff and Money. *Legal Times,* v. 9, January 26, 1987. pp. 1,8.

[241] One political scientist, who monitored the Judiciary Committee throughout 1979, said the creation of a special investigative team within the committee provided much better information about nominees than in the past, when "the committee in a sense was always prisoner to information coming from elsewhere." Cohodas, Nadine. Kennedy and Rodino: How Two Very Different

concludes in late June or early July, when the Court goes into recess for the next three months. The five most recent Justices to retire from the Court –Potter Stewart (in 1981), Warren Burger (In 1986), Lewis Powell (in 1987), William Brennan (in 1990) and Thurgood Marshall (in 1991) – announced their retirements in either late June or July, at the end or approaching end of the court's term.

Highly relevant to when each of these vacancies could be filled was the working calendar of the Senate, for in little more than a month of each Supreme Court retirement the Senate was scheduled to take its customary month-long summer recess in August. Receipt from the President of a Supreme Court nomination in late June or early or mid-July presented the Judiciary Committee with the choices of holding confirmation hearings prior to the August recess, during the recess, or in September after the Senate reconvened. Even if the Committee chose, on an expedited basis, to hold hearings prior to the August recess, there would be little or almost no time left before the recess for the Senate as a whole to consider the nomination. Thus, in 1986, although the Judiciary Committee held confirmation hearings on (and reported out) the Rehnquist and Antonin Scalia nominations just prior the August recess, the Senate did not conduct its floor debate on the nominations until after the recess, in mid-September. In contrast to its handling of the Rehnquist and Scalia nominations, the Judiciary Committee, after receiving the nominations of Robert H. Bork (1987), David H. Souter (1990) and Clarence Thomas (1991) in July, scheduled those confirmation hearings for September, *after* the August recess,[242] and Senate debate on each of these nominations began in October.[243]

The appropriate overall length of time to be taken by the confirmation process became an issue in 1987 during Senate consideration of the Bork nomination. On July 1, 1987 President Ronald Reagan announced that he would nominate Robert

---

Chairman Run Their Panels. *Congressional Quarterly Weekly Report,* v. 38, February 2, 1980. p. 269 (quoting Elliot Slotnick, assistant professor of political science, Ohio State University).

242 The length of time between Senate receipt of nomination and start of confirmation hearings was 70 days for Judge Bork, 50 days for Judge Souter, and 64 days for Judge Thomas.

243 Television, it may be argued, is also a factor which has contributed to the increasing length of the Supreme Court confirmation process. Since 1981, when nominee Sandra Day O'Connor appeared to testify, the Judiciary committee has allowed every Supreme Court confirmation hearing to be televised. Also, since 1986, when the Senate opened its floor proceedings to television, floor debate on every Supreme court nomination has received extensive coverage by the broadcast and cable television media. The certainty that they will be watched by millions of American television viewers presents the Senate Judiciary Committee and the Senate with an opportunity to "showcase" their deliberations. This, it may be argued, provides an incentive for the Committee and the Senate not only to take greater time in preparing for hearings and floor debate than they would if these deliberations were closed to television, but also to schedule lengthier hearings and debate.

H. Bork to fill the vacancy created by the retirement of Associated Justice Lewis F. Powell, Jr. on June 26, 1987. Within days of the President's announcement, Senate Democrats and Republicans found themselves in sharp disagreement over when the Senate Judiciary Committee should start its hearings on the Bork nomination. The final authority on this question rested with the Democratic chairman of the Committee, Senator Biden, who in early July designated September 15, 1987 as the starting date for the Bork hearings.[244]

At various points during the ensuing weeks of July, Senate Republicans and Democrats debated whether September 15 was soon enough to begin confirmation hearings. Favoring earlier hearings, some Republicans attacked the September 15 start-up date, calling it part of a Democratic strategy of stalling. President Reagan joined in the criticisms, maintaining that because hearings would not start until mid-September the Supreme Court would have a vacancy and be at less than full strength when its term began on October 5, 1987. Senate Democrats defended the schedule set for the Bork hearings and denied accusations of trying to stall the confirmation process. They argued that, in light of the controversy surrounding the Bork nomination, Committee staff and Members needed the time that had been reserved prior to the scheduled start of hearings to study the nominee's record adequately.[245]

In answer to persisting Republican allegations that Senate Democrats might extend the hearings indefinitely, Chairman Biden in early August 1987 announced his objective of having the Bork nomination come to a Judiciary Committee vote by October 1.[246] After holding 12 days of hearings, the Committee voted to report the Bork nomination, with a negative recommendation, on October 6, 1987. Two and a half weeks later, on October 23, 1987, the Senate, after three days of debate, rejected the Bork nomination by a vote of 58 to 42. This final action came 108 days after Senate receipt of the President's nomination.

Four years later, almost as much time – 99 days – elapsed between President George Bush's nomination of Clarence Thomas on July 8, 1991 and the Senate's confirmation of the nominee on October 15, 1991. Members of the Senate disagreed among themselves on whether it was appropriate for the confirmation process to have taken so long. Some suggested that the process was unfair and cruel in allowing the nominee and his reputation to be public targets for attack by opponents for such a length of time. During the final day of Senate debate on the Thomas nomination, for instance, Minority Leader Bob Dole commented that Judge Thomas "for 107 days has been hanging out there twisting in the wind

---

[244] See Rutkus, *Senate Consideration of Bork nomination* (see footnote 203), pp. 11-14.

[245] *Ibid.*

[246] *Ibid.*

while every effort conceivable, every effort known to man was used to discredit him and defeat his nomination."[247] Similarly, Senator John C. Danforth declared that "no human being ever should have to go through what Clarence Thomas has gone through for the last 100-plus days, and particularly for the last 10 days."[248]

Others, however, maintained that the lifetime nature of a Supreme Court appointment justified an extended inquiry into the qualifications of a nominee to the Court. The Senate, Senator Biden has argued, was particularly entitled to be deliberate when the appointment involved a relatively youthful nominee, such as the 43-year-old Clarence Thomas, who conceivably might serve on the Court for as many as 40 years:

> We will hear discussion today, I suspect, about whether or not 100 days is an inordinate amount of time to have this nomination under consideration.
> I would point out that if we confirm this nominee, we are talking about 15,000 days-15,000 days-that he will be making decisions that will affect our lives.[249]

During the October 15, 1991 debate, Majority Leader George J. Mitchell joined Senator Biden in defending the time taken by the Senate to process the Thomas nomination. He contrasted the Thomas confirmation process, leading to an actual Senate vote on the nomination, with the 1968 Senate battle over the nomination of Abe Fortas to be Chief Justice – the last Supreme Court nomination by a Democratic President. In that episode, a filibuster effectively had blocked a Senate vote on the Fortas nomination.[250]

---

[247] Dole, Bob. Nomination of Clarence Thomas, of Georgia, To Be an Associate Justice of the Supreme Court of the United States. Remarks in the Senate. *Congressional Record,* Daily Edition, v. 137, October 15, 1991. p. S14702. In alluding to 107 days Senator Dole evidently started his count of the overall confirmation process from the data that President Bush announced his choice of Judge Thomas to be his nominee (July I, 1991) rather than the date on which he actually sent the Thomas nomination to the Senate (July 8, 1991).

[248] Danfoth, John C. Nomination of Clarence Thomas, of Georgia, To Be an Associate Justice of the Supreme Court of the United States. Remarks in the Senate. *Congressional Record,* Daily Edition, v. 137, October 15, 1991. p. S14702.

[249] Biden, Joseph R., Jr. Nomination of Clarence Thomas, of Georgia, To Be an Associate Justice of the Supreme Court of the United States. Remarks in the Senate. *Congressional Record,* Daily Edition, v. 137, October 15, 1991. p. S14627.

[250] "In the nomination now before us," Senator Mitchell remarked, "our Republican colleagues have repeatedly said that 100 days to consider it is too long. But the last time the situation was reversed, they wanted a delay of 7 months to even begin consideration of the nomination." Senator Mitchell recalled that when President Lyndon B. Johnson in June of 1968 nominated then-Justice Fortas to be Chief Justice, 19 republican Senators issued a statement (a portion of which Senator Mitchell introduced into the *Congressional Record)* expressing the "strongly held view" of the 19 Senators that "any nominees for the vacancies on the Supreme Court should be selected by the newly elected President of the United States, after the people have expressed

Subsequent to the above events, differing reform measures were proposed for shortening the appointments process. One proposal came from President Bush, who found fault with the length of time taken by the Senate in confirming Presidential nominations in general. The Senate, President Bush urged, should "shorten the time-lapse between nominations and confirmation; shorten it to 6 weeks."[251]

A contrasting perspective, however, soon was forthcoming from the Senate Democratic Task Force on the Confirmation Process. In its report the Task Force focused on actions that it said should be taken by the *executive* branch. "To speed the confirmation process," the Task Force recommended, "the Executive Branch should submit nominations promptly when a vacancy occurs, streamline and expedite its investigative process, and certify that nominees are fit for confirmation."[252]

At issue between the two sides was whether efforts to shorten the appointments process should focus only on the Senate confirmation phase or also on Presidential selection phase. During the Reagan and Bush presidencies, the time taken by the President in the pre-nomination phase was often a sizable part of the overall appointment process for judgeships to lower Federal courts (as well as for appointive positions in the executive branch); many of these judgeships had remained vacant for months (and some for years) before nominees were selected and sent to the Senate.[253] By contrast, Presidents Reagan and Bush almost always

---

themselves in November's elections." The purpose of the 19 Members' expressed preference for delay on Supreme Court appointments until the swearing in of a new President in January 1969, Senator Mitchell asserted, was "to defeat the [Fortas] nomination. And they did, even though a majority of Senators favored the nomination." Mitchell, George J. Nomination of Clarence Thomas, of Georgia, To be an Associate Justice of the Supreme Court of the United States. Remarks in the Senate. *Congressional Record,* Daily Edition, v. 137, October 15, 1991, pp. S14702-03.

The filibuster strategy against the Fortas nomination proved successful when a motion to close debate failed to gain the necessary two-thirds majority of those Senate Members voting. (The roll call vote in favor of cloture was 45 to 43.) At the time of the cloture vote, on October I, 1968, The Fortas nomination had been pending in the Senate for 97 days. See: Attempt To Stop Fortas Debate Fails by 14-Vote Margin. *Congressional Quarterly Weekly Report,* v. 26, October 4, 1968. p. 2613.

[251] To make his case for shortening the process, President Bush compared the present with the past: "it takes four times as long to secure a vote today; four times as long as it did just 30 years ago, during the Presidency of John Kennedy. It took the Senate an average of 63 days to confirm our appointments sent up in 1989; 65 days for the group nominated in 1990. We now have a large group of people waiting for the Senate to vote on their nominations, and they have been waiting an average of 80 days." Bush, Remarks to Public Administration Groups, p. 1497.

[252] Democratic Task Force, Report (see footnote 14), p. S898.

[253] Senator Mitchell emphasized this point on floor remarks discussing the findings of the Senate Democratic Task Force on the Confirmation Process. "The task force report," he said, "shows that an average of 350 days – almost a year – passes between the creation of a vacancy and the

selected Supreme Court nominees quickly, within days of a vacancy being created on the Court.[254]

Meanwhile, at least one legal commentator has questioned whether quick selection by the President actually helps shorten the Supreme Court appointment process overall. A Supreme Court nomination quickly made, according to this commentator, is in effect a "surprise" which should be avoided. Announced without any advance notice, the nomination thereafter undergoes background investigations by the Federal Bureau of Investigation, the American Bar Association's Standing Committee on the Federal Judiciary, and Senate committee investigators, followed by hearings of the Senate Judiciary Committee. Whereas the President has acted "quickly in naming his choice," the Senate "plod[s] through months of deliberations."[255]

This "allocation of time," the commentator maintains, "should be substantially reversed" – with much more time allocated to the pre-nomination phase. The White House, he has proposed, should avoid surprises and publicly announce a list of three to five candidates from which the Supreme Court nominee would be chosen. Each candidate would be investigated by the FBI, the ABA and Senate investigators (as well as by the press), and perhaps also interviewed personally by the President.[256] Adding these weeks to the pre-nomination phase, the commentator suggests, could actually shorten the overall appointments process. To demonstrate this, he has provided the following scenario:

> Most Supreme Court vacancies are created at the end of the Court's term in late June or early July. The Court does not resume sitting until October. ...

Senate's conformation of a nominee to fill that position. But of these 350 days, about 270 pass, on average, while waiting for the President to determine whom he will nominate." Mitchell George J. Remarks in the Senate. *Congressional Record,* Daily Edition, v. 138, February 4, 1992. p. S893.

[254] In one instance, President Reagan, a few days after a Supreme Court vacancy was created, announced his *intention* to nominate someone to the Supreme Court, only to wait for 43 days thereafter before actually sending the nomination to the Senate. On July 7, 1981, four days after Justice Potter Stewart retired from the Court, President Reagan announced his intention to nominate Sandra Jay O'Connor to succeed Justice Stewart. Mr. Reagan said he would send the nomination to the Senate "upon completion of all the necessary checks by the Federal Bureau of Investigation. ..." U.S. President, 1991-89 (Reagan). Supreme Court of the United States, July 7, 1981. *Weekly Compilation of Presidential Documents,* v. 17, July 13, 1981. p. 729. Subsequently, six weeks passed before the nomination was submitted to the Senate on August 19, 1981. For more discussion of the delay in this phase of the Connor nomination process, see U.S. Library of Congress. Congressional Research Service. *The Speed with Which Action Has Been Taken on Supreme Court Nominations in the Last 25 Years.* Report 87-576 GOV, by Denis Steven Rutkus. Washington, D.C., 1987. p. 4.

[255] Tofel, Four Steps (see footnote 29), pp. 22, 26.

[256] *Ibid.*, p. 22.

> Particularly if the names of possible nominees were publicly available early on, a president would be right to insist on a schedule something like this: hearings commencing within one week of a nomination, lasting no more than two weeks, with a vote within one week thereafter. If such a vote had been scheduled for September 30 this year [1991], to enable the nominee to participate fully in the Court's new term, no nomination would have been necessary until September 3.[257]

The same sentiments have been expressed by Senator Paul Simon, a Member of the Judiciary Committee. Senator Simon faulted President Bush for announcing the Clarence Thomas nomination five days after Justice Thurgood Marshall announced his retirement. Presidents generally "have served the nation best," Senator Simon maintained, "by taking time to look over the legal landscape carefully" in search of a person to fill a Supreme Court vacancy. "A delay of thirty days or sixty days," the Senator continued, "would at least give the appearance of thoughtfulness, but I hope it would give the nation much more than simply the appearance."[258]

CONCLUSION

The question of Clarence Thomas's fitness to serve on the Supreme Court, while ultimately decided by the Senate, left another unresolved question in its wale – whether the Supreme Court appointment process should be reformed. Unhappy with the way in which the process had worked during the Thomas confirmation battle, Members of Congress, political scientists, legal scholars, media commentators and others offered a wide variety of reform proposals. The ensuing debate over what reforms to adopt, has resulted in very few areas of agreement.

Critics of the appointment process have differed sharply on what aspects of that process are most in need of change. Some have focused their attention on the process by which the President selects a nominee. Others have called for reform of the way in which the Senate Judiciary Committee investigates the background and qualifications of the nominee. Still others have proposed restricting the involvement of outside interest groups in the appointment process, or shortening the overall length of time taken by the process.

---

[257] *Ibid.*, p. 26.

[258] Simon, *Advice & Consent* (see footnote 157), pp. 309-10.

Various approaches to reform have in themselves been controversial by virtue of calling on the President or the Senate to relinquish or share powers on the appointment process that each now exercises exclusively. Reform proposals affecting the President have included calls on the Chief Executive to consult with the Senate before selecting a nominee, to use criteria set by the Senate in evaluating prospective nominees, or to make the selection process more open to the Senate and the public. Other proposals would restrain or regulate the Senate in the performance of its "advice and consent" role. In this category are proposals to limit the scope of the Judiciary Committee's staff investigations, require that advance notice be provided to the nominee of what questions will be posed at confirmation hearings, limit the repetitiousness and length of Committee questioning of the nominee, and require the Senate, after having received the President's nomination, to take final action within a set period of time.

An initial challenge in addressing many reform issues, of course, is to achieve bipartisan agreement or support for a particular course of action. This especially can be difficult when Senators of the President's party perceive that a proposed reform would encroach upon the President's nominating power or inject into the confirmation process new risks for the nominee. Achieving a particular change (especially in the nominating process) might also require cooperation from the executive branch, yet realistically such cooperation might be unattainable if it would constitute a weakening of Presidential prerogatives or power.[259]

Other dimensions of the appointment process not directly involving the President might also be beyond the Senate's power to change. It can be argued, for instance, that it would be impossible for any reform measure to insure that unethical conduct by a Senate employee or Member would not take place in the appointment process or that such conduct would not escape unpunished. Senate reform might also be hard-pressed to curb unethical activities by outside interest groups, such as untruthful issue advertising in the media designed to influence the outcome of the appointment process.[260]

---

[259] Some particularly have expressed skepticism about the Senate's ability to reform the *nomination* process. "The nomination process, say former attorneys general and White House counsel, cannot be improved because there are no objective standards. It cannot be formalized, they add, because if it did not produce the choice sought by the president, the chief executive would ignore it." Coyle, Marcia, and Fred Strasser. Changing Times Benefit [Anthony M.] Kennedy. *National Law Journal,* v. 10, November 23, 1987. p. 29.

[260] See Biden, Joseph R., Jr. Nomination of Clarence Thomas, of Georgia, To Be An Associate Justice of the Supreme Court of the United States. Remarks in the Senate. *Congressional Record,* Daily Edition, v. 147, October 15, 1991. p. S14627 (discussing the inability of the Senate to "absolutely prevent or control" unethical conduct that a Senator, a Senate staff member or outside interest groups might engage in).

Certain aspects of the appointment process also might be difficult to alter because they are inherent to the process. This especially might be the case for the political nature of the process, which often becomes highly pronounced when a President submits a controversial nomination or when there are sharp partisan or ideological differences between the President and the Senate.[261] Indeed, to seek, by way or reform, to "correct" the political aspects of the process, one Member of the Senate Judiciary Committee has suggested, may work at cross purposes with the Constitution.[262]

Perhaps also not lending themselves to reform would be personal prerogatives individual Senators historically have exercised in the appointment process. Illustrative are the criteria that Senators use to evaluate the fitness of a Supreme Court nominee to serve on the Court. As indicated earlier, Senators vary in the relative importance they ascribe to different kinds of criteria, and the actual criteria used in evaluating a Supreme Court nominee typically have been a personal, very individual matter for each Senator. [263] Hence, it might be impractical for the Senate to attempt to establish any criteria designed to be binding upon all of its Members.

Nevertheless, reform of the Supreme Court appointment process is not impossible, and in fact, since the confirmation of the Clarense Thomas nomination in October 1991, reform has occurred in the Senate in two areas. One set of reforms has clarified and altered the nature of the access which Senate Members and Senate staff are afforded to confidential background information

---

[261] The historic record supports the argument that adversary politics is a recurring, if not built-in, feature of the Supreme Court appointment process. "Of the 144 Supreme Court nominees prior to Judge Thomas," one scholar has observed, "27 (nearly one out of five) have been rejected, withdrawn, or not acted on by the Senate. The importance of political partisanship is undeniable. When the president and Senate majority have been of the same party, consent has been given to more than 90 per cent of the nominations. When they have been of different parties, more than half the nominees have not been confirmed." Feingold, Stanley. Sure It's Politics; When Wasn't it? *National Law Journal,* v. 13, September 2, 1991. p. 18.

[262] Senator Dennis DeConcini notes that the Constitution has assigned the responsibility for filling Supreme Court vacancies to the Government's two "political branches" – the Presidency and the Senate. In doing so, he maintains, "the Constitution foresaw the political friction that has been a part of this process since the beginning." He adds that the "political element of this process can be distasteful at times as can the politics of any other policy issue. Corrections to the process are needed but true reform will not be achieved by ignoring the fundamental nature of this process." DeConcini, Examining the Process (see footnote 27), p. 24.

[263] See earlier section of this report under the heading "Criteria Used by Senate" (where it was noted that in the past some Senators have attached greatest weight to a nominee's professional qualifications, others have stressed the importance of the nominee's judicial philosophy or views on constitutional issues, while still others have indicated that they have been influenced in varying degrees by both kinds of criteria.)

about Supreme Court nominees maintained by the Judiciary Committee.[264] These reforms have been put into effect by joint action of the Committee Chairman and Ranking Minority Member[265] as well as by the Chairman acting in his individual capacity.[266]

Another reform instituted by the Chairman of the Judiciary Committee has addressed the issue of when, if ever, to close Supreme Court confirmation hearings. Under a new procedure announced by the Chairman, closed Judiciary Committee sessions, during his chairmanship, will be scheduled for Supreme Court nominees to respond to any investigative charges that have been filed with the committee.[267]

The actions just noted occurred under certain conditions that were relatively favorable to the implementation of reform. The issue of Senate Member and Committee staff access to FBI background information about Supreme Court nominees, while highly sensitive (because of the "leaks" of the Anita Hill allegations against Clarence Thomas), was resolved with an arrangement on February 7, 1992 that had the unanimous, bi-partisan support of the Members of the Judiciary Committee; a new memorandum of understanding signed that day reinstated a longstanding arrangement between the President and the Senate Judiciary Committee, while adding certain clarifications – thus, constituting no diminution of either the executive's or the Senate's powers in the appointment process.

Similarly, the establishment by the Judiciary Committee Chairman of a new procedure allowing all 100 Senators to inspect all confidential documents and reports compiled by the Committee on Supreme Court nominees, and the Chairman's announcement that closed committee sessions will routinely be held for future nominees, generated no conflict between the political parties or balance of power issues between the White House and the Senate. Absent such conflicts,

---

[264] See earlier section of this report under the heading "Access to Confidential Information."

[265] On February a7, 1992, the Chairman and the Ranking Minority Member of the Senate Judiciary Committee signed a new memorandum of understanding with the White House, making access to FBI files on judicial nominees once again available to designated Committee staff as well as to Senators on the Committee. (Three month earlier, on October 14, 1991, President Bush had limited this access to Senators only.) The memo also contained new clarifications regarding security measures to be taken by the Judiciary Committee to ensure the confidentiality of FBI information in the Committee's possession.

[266] On June 25, 1992, Chairman Biden announced in a Senate floor speech that he was instituting new procedures governing confidential information, under which confidential non-FBI documents and reports compiled by the Committee on future Supreme Court nominees would be available for inspection by all 100 Senators. Biden, Reform of the Confirmation Process (see footnote 18), p. S8866.

[267] Biden, Reform of Confirmation Process (see footnote 18) p. S8866. Also see earlier section of this report, under the heading "When Hearings Should Be Closed."

the latter two reform actions concerned the prerogatives of a Committee chairman solely in a Senate Context.

In future Senate debates over whether to undertake further reform of the Supreme court appointment process, a useful starting point might be to recognize the existence of a number of commonly held values or goals. For example, most critics of the appointment process, among other things, should:

- result in appointment to the Supreme Court of persons meeting the highest standards of integrity and professional competence;
- bring to light all information relevant to the issue of a nominee's qualifications and fitness to serve on the Court;
- bolster rather than undermine public confidence in the three branches of the Federal Government; and
- promote the Supreme Court's judicial integrity and its constitutional independence of the executive and legislative branches.

Beyond such a starting point, however, the following questions arise: Are there other basic purposes, besides those noted above, that the Supreme Court appointment process should achieve? Has the appointment process satisfactorily fulfilled its basic purposes in recent years? If not, what reforms of the process are called for, if any?

During the 102nd Congress, the Senate debated at length what actions should be taken to reform the Supreme Court appointment process in light of various difficulties experienced during the Thomas confirmation battle of 1991.

During the 103rd Congress, a policy question for the Senate will be whether to reexamine the appointment process, and again consider available reform options, before a new vacancy is created on the Supreme Court.

APPENDIX: A CHRONOLOGY OF SELECTED EVENTS RELEVANT TO THE SUPREME COURT APPOINTMENT PROCESS, OCTOBER 15, 1991 TO THE PRESENT

October 15, 1991. The U.S. Senate votes, 52 to 48, to confirm the nomination of Clarence Thomas of Georgia to be an Associate Justice on the Supreme Court, the 48 nays constituting the most votes ever cast against a nominee confirmed to the Court. In Senate floor debate preceding the confirmation vote, various Members criticize the Supreme Court confirmation process, calling for reform.[268] Senator Paul Simon of Illinois introduces S. Res.194, expressing the sense of the Senate that in determining whom to name to any future Supreme Court vacancies, the President should "keep philosophical balance in mind" and engage in "informal, bipartisan consultation with some members of the Senate" before submitting a nomination to the Senate. The resolution is referred to the Senate Judiciary Committee.[269]

October 22, 1991. Senate Majority Leader George J. Mitchell names Senator Wendell H. Ford of Kentucky to head a task force of five Senate committee chairmen to examine the confirmation process and make recommendations.[270]

October 24, 1991. President George Bush urges that various actions be taken to reform the Senate confirmation process: First, that the time lapse between nominations and confirmation be shortened to six weeks; second, that access to FBI reports on nominees which are sent to the Senate be limited to Senators only (and no longer be afforded to Senate staff), to ensure the confidentiality of those reports; third, that the Senate appoint a special counsel to investigate the unauthorized "leaks" to the news media of allegations against Clarence Thomas which law professor Anita Hill earlier had supplied to the Senate Judiciary Committee on a confidential basis; (4) fourth, that more "tolerant, less viciously partisan debate" over nominations be promoted.[271]

---

[268] U.S. Congress. Senate. Executive Session; Nomination of Clarence Thomas, of Georgia, To be An Associate Justice of the Supreme Court of the Unites States. *Congressional Record,* Daily Edition, v. 137, October 15, 1991. pp. S14626-705.

[269] U.S. Congress. Senate. Senate Resolution 194 – Relative to Appointments to the United States Supreme Court. *Congressional Record,* v. 137, October 15, 1991. p. S14712-13.

[270] In addition to Senator Ford, Chairman of the Rules and Administration Committee, the task force consists of Senators Joseph R. Biden, Jr. (Judiciary Committee), Claiborne Pell (Foreign Relations Committee), Sam Nunn (Armed Services Committee), and David L. Boren (Select Committee in Intelligence). See Alston, Chuck. Bush Takes Congress to Task; Democrats Fire Right Back. *Congressional Quarterly Weekly Report,* v. 49. October 26, 1991. pp. 3106-07.

[271] Bush, Remarks to Public Administration Groups (see footnote 63), pp. 1495-500.

On the same day, the Senate by a vote of 86 to 12 approves a resolution appointing a special counsel to investigate the unauthorized disclosures of Professor Hill's allegations against Clarence Thomas. The resolution, S. Res. 202, also mandates that the special counsel investigate disclosures of non-public confidential information from Senate documents in connection with the Select Committee on Ethics investigation of matters relating to savings and loan executive Charles Keating. The resolution directs the special counsel, within 120 days of appointment, to transmit a report of finding to the Senate Majority and Minority leaders. Further, the resolution provides that the Majority Leader and the Minority Leader, after receipt of the special counsel's report, will make "recommendations for any change in Federal law or in Senate rules that should be made to prevent similar unauthorized disclosures in the future."[272]

November 21, 1991. The Judiciary Committee unanimously passes a resolution calling on President Bush to rescind his order of the month before which bars Senate investigative stall from seeing FBE report material on nominees. The bipartisan consensus on the Judiciary Committee is that access to FBI material for designated staff is essential to the Committee in performing an investigative role in the confirmation process.[273]

February 4, 1992. Majority Leader Mitchell issues the report of the Senate Democratic Task Force on the Confirmation Process. Among other things, the Task Force report urges that consultations be initiated immediately between the President and Senate leaders on future Supreme Court nominations. "Such consultations," the Task Force maintains, "would minimize conflict between the two branches, and expedite the confirmation process." The Task Force also calls on the executive branch to "streamline and expedite" its process for investigating nominees, so that all relevant information will be forwarded to the Senate at the same time that the President submits a nomination to the Senate. Further, the Task Force urges the Administration to restore earlier arrangements whereby designated Senate committee staff members were allowed access to confidential FBI background information on nominees.[274]

---

[272] Resolution Relative to the Appointment of Special Counsel-Senate Resolution 202. *Congressional Record,* Daily Edition, v. 137, October 24, 1991. pp. S15122-34.

[273] Simpson, Judiciary Tells Bush (see footnote 67), pp. 1, 21.

[274] Without a restoration of those arrangements, the Task Force warns, the Senate committees would be compelled to expand their own investigative staff and duplicate investigative work already done by the FBI; this in turn, the Task Force predicts, would have the undesirable consequence of further prolonging the confirmation process. U.S. Congress. Senate. Report of the Task Force on the Confirmation Process. *Congressional Record,* Daily Edition, v. 138, February 4, 1992. pp. S895-98.

February 7, 1992. The white House and Senate Judiciary Committee settle their dispute over access to FBI reports. A new memorandum of understanding[275] reinstates the 1989 White House – Judiciary Committee agreement which President Bush had rescinded the previous October. Under the new understanding, access to FBI files on judicial nominees again will be available to designated committee staff as well as to Senators on the Committee.[276]

May 5, 1992. Peter Fleming, the Senate special counsel, reports to the Senate on his investigation into the unauthorized release to the news media of Anita Hill's sexual harassment allegations against Clarence Thomas.[277] The highly detailed report concludes that the document released to the press without authorization was not an FBI report of interviews with Professor Hill but rather had originated in the Senate. The report adds, however, that its investigation has been unable to identify the Senate source of the "leaked" information.[278]

June 25, 1992. Senator Joseph R. Biden, Jr., the Chairmen of the Judiciary Committee, delivers an extended speech on the floor of the Senate concerning reform of the Supreme Court appointment process.[279] In his speech he declares:

> A legitimate process that was built in good faith to identify and confirm consensus nominees has been destroyed by many of the same corrosive influences that have so devastated our Presidential politics and our national dialog on public affairs.
> Consequently, it is my view that – particularly if the reality of divided government during a time of great change at the Court continues in the next administration – future confirmations must be conducted differently than the preceding ones. The pressures and tensions on the existing process – which exploded during the Thomas nomination fight – make restoration of what

[275] The memorandum is signed by the White House counsel to the President, the Chairman of the Judiciary Committee and the Committee's Ranking Minority Member.

[276] In a concession to the President, however, the memo adds certain clarifications. It stipulates that: 1) document control experts from Senate security periodically will review the effectiveness of procedures used to maintain physical custody of files; 2) photocopying or verbatim reproduction of FBI reports will be prohibited; and 3) Committee notes and memoranda on FBI Files will be secured in a manner identical to FBI report. *Ibid.*

[277] Also, the special counsel, in accordance with his mandate from the Senate, reports on his investigation into the unauthorized release to the news media of confidential Ethics Committee information relating to savings and loan executive Charles Keating.

[278] U.S. Senate. *Report of Temporary Special Independent Counsel Pursuant to Senate Resolution 202.* Senate Document No. 102-20, Part 1, 102d Cong., 2d Sess. Washington, U.S. Govt. Print. Off., 1992. pp. 2-3. The report also reports that it can "find no basis for criticizing the procedures of the Judiciary Committee or otherwise attributing the [Anita] Hill disclosures to any shortcomings in its internal practices." *Ibid.*, p. 73.

[279] Biden, Reform of Confirmation Process (see footnote 18), pp. S8853-67.

came before Judge Thomas' nomination – even it if it was desirable – a practical impossibility.[280]

Chairman Biden proposes four major changes in the Supreme Court appointment process: First, he urges that whenever there is "divided Government" (between a President of one party and a Senate majority of the other party), the President should engage in genuine consultation with the Senate on Supreme Court nominations or, instead, appoint nominees who philosophically stride the "middle ground between the parties." Second, he maintains, the Senate should be more active than it has been in the past in using the pre-hearing phase of the confirmation process for debate relating to the philosophy of the nominee. Third, he asserts, the hearings of the Judiciary Committee should be used to explore fully the nominee's judicial philosophy, and Members should feel free to oppose a nominee who does not answer questions that they believe should be answered. Fourth, Senator Biden announces new Judiciary committee procedures will be instituted to improve public confidence in the committee's handling of confidential investigative material concerning the nominee.[281]

Immediately thereafter, Senator Strom Thurmond, the Ranking Minority Member of the Judiciary Committee, responds to Senator Biden's speech. Senator Thurmond asserts that under Article II of the Constitution, it is the President, "not the majority leader, the minority leader, chairman or ranking member of the Judiciary Committee who has the responsibility for putting forth a supreme Court nominee." To require a President "to seek and obtain the approval of a small but vocal minority of Senators and special interest groups who have failed to defeat his previous nominees, "Senator Thurmond maintains, "would turn the current nomination process on its head."[282]

August 11, 1992. In San Francisco, at its annual convention, the American Bar Association's House of Delegates votes 276 to 168 in favor of a resolution supporting a woman's right to have an abortion.[283] The ABA action prompts 23 organizations of politically conservative orientation, in a letter to Attorney General William Barr, to demand that the ABA's Standing Committee on the

[280] *Ibid.*, p. S8862.
[281] *Ibid.*, pp. S8863-66.
[282] Thurmond, Strom. Response to Senator Biden's Remarks on the Confirmation Process of Supreme Court Nominees. *Congressional Record,* Daily Edition, v. 138, June 25, 1992. p. S8867.
[283] See Torry, Saundra. Lawyers' Group Votes To Back Abortion Rights. *Washington Post,* August 12, 1992. p. A14.

Federal Judiciary be stripped of its longstanding role as evaluator of judicial candidates for the Justice Department and for the Senate Judiciary Committee.[284]

November 3, 1992. (Election Day). Democratic candidate Bill Clinton is elected the 42nd President of the United States, defeating George Bush, the Republican incumbent. At the same time, congressional election returns enable the Democrats to retain their majority status in both the U.S. House of Representative and the Senate. The ranks of the Senate Democrats include four newly elected women, all of whom during their campaigns for the Senate had criticized the all-male makeup of the Judiciary Committee and the Committee's handling of sexual harassment allegations against Supreme Court nominee Clarence Thomas during October 1991 hearings on the Matter.[285] The election results mean that starting in early 1993, for the first time in seven years, the party in control of the Senate will be receiving judicial nominations from a President of the same party.[286]

January 7, 1993. At the start of the 103d Congress, two women are named to the formerly all-male Senate Judiciary Committee. Appointed to the Committee by the Senate Democratic Caucus are Senators Carol Moseley Braun (D-IL) and Dianne Feinstein (D-CA), both newly elected Senate Members. A few days

[284] Roman, Nancy E. Conservatives: ABA Bias Taints Judge-Approval Role. *Washington Times,* August 14, 1992. p. A3.

[285] See Katz, Jeffrey L., and Ceci Connolly. Women, Minorities Rock Records, But Ideology Will Barely Budge.

[286] During President Bush's four years in office (1989-92), and during the last two years of the Reagan Presidency, (1987-88), opposing parties shared control of the judicial appointment process-that is, a Republican President nominated Federal judges, while the Democrats were the majority party in the Senate and Thus held effective control of the judicial confirmation process. By contrast, the sane party was in control of both the White House and the Senate during the Presidency of Democrat Jimmy Carter (1977-80) and during the first six years of the Presidency of Republican Ronald Reagan (1981-86).

earlier, the Chairman of the Judiciary Committee, Senator Biden, had expressed his intention to recruit one or two of the Senate's four newly elected female Members to serve on the Committee.[287]

[287] Dewar, Helen. Feinstein and Braun end Male Rule on Senate Judiciary Committee. *Washington Post,* January 7, 1993. p. A8. Neibuhr, Gustav. Women Recruited for Judiciary Panel. *Washington Post,* January 4, 1993. p. A5.

Chapter 3

PROFESSIONAL QUALIFICATIONS FOR APPOINTMENT TO THE FEDERAL JUDICIARY

P.L. Morgan

A question frequently presented is whether there is a requirement that federal judges be lawyers. The answer is that there are no constitutional provisions setting forth professional qualifications for appointees to the judiciary. The very few statutory professional prerequisites apply only to nominees to federal courts whose judges are not constitutionally entitled to "good Behaviour" tenure.[1] Thus, judges of the United States Tax Court are appointed "solely on the grounds of fitness to perform the duties of office," 26 *U.S.C.* § 7443; judges of the local court system of the District of Columbia must meet certain bar membership and practice qualifications, 11 *D.C. Code* § 1501; and judges of the United States Court of Military Appeals, the United States Court of Veterans Appeals, bankruptcy courts, and United States Magistrates must meet certain bar membership qualifications, 10 *U.S.C* § 867, 38 *U.S.C* § 7253, 28 *U.S.C.* §§ 153 note, 631.

---

[1] Judges appointed to federal courts established under Article III of the Constitution, *i.e.*, the Supreme Court, United States Courts of Appeals, United States District courts, and the United States Court of International Trade, have "good Behaviour" tenure. Judges of these courts may only be removed from office three ways: voluntarily by relinquishing office; involuntarily by impeachment; or upon death. The remainder of the federal courts are established under constitutional authority with judges appointed for a set term of years as authorized by Congress.

APPARENT INTENT OF THE FRAMERS OF THE CONSTITUTION

It seems evident that lawyers were intended to fill federal judgeships as early as the 1787 Philadelphia Convention held preparatory to adoption of a federal constitution. These germane comments have been reported:

> Dr. FRANKLIN observed, that two modes of choosing the judges had been mentioned — *to wit,* by the legislature and by the executive. He wished such other modes to be suggested as might occur to other gentlemen; it being a point of great moment. He would mention one which he understood was practised in Scotland. He then, in a brief and entertaining manner, related a Scotch mode, in which the nomination proceeded from the lawyers, who always selected the ablest of the profession, in order to get rid of him, and share his practice among themselves. ...Elliot, *V Debates on the Adoption of the Federal Constitution* 156 (1888) [Debate of June 5, 1787].
>
> Mr. MADISON objected to an appointment by the whole legislature. Many of them are incompetent judges of the requisite qualifications. They were too much influenced by their partialities. The candidate who was present, who had displayed a talent for business in the legislative field, who had, perhaps, assisted ignorant members in business of their own or of their constituents, or used other winning means, would, without any of the essential qualifications for an expositor of the laws, prevail over a competitor not having these recommendations, but possessed of every necessary accomplishment. ...*Id.* at 188 [Debate of June 13, 1787].

Additional indicia of the framer's intent may be found in *The Federalist,* Number 78, authored by Alexander Hamilton. That work, composed of eighty five compositions, was published anonymously under the pseudonym "Publius" during the debate over adoption of the Constitution. Printed in New York newspapers, the articles were written by Hamilton, John Jay and James Madison, all proponents of the instrument. The germane portions of the composition, which seem to suggest that judges were to be selected from the ranks of lawyers, provide:

> ...To avoid an arbitrary discretion in the courts, it is indispensable that they should be bound down by strict rules and precedents, which serve to define and point out their duty in every particular case that comes before them; and it will readily be conceived from the variety of controversies which grow out of the folly and wickedness of mankind, that the records of those precedents must unavoidably swell to a very considerable bulk, and must demand long and laborious study to acquire a competent knowledge of them. Hence it is, that there can be but few men in the society who will have sufficient skill in

> the laws to qualify them for the stations of judges. ...a temporary duration in office, which would naturally discourage such characters from quitting a lucrative line of practice to accept a seat on the bench. ...

Early Congressional Discussions Relative to Judicial Qualifications

During Congressional debate just subsequent to ratification of the Constitution, participants appear to be speaking of judges with the understanding that they were lawyers. In January 1801, the following debate was reported when an amendment was introduced to change a salary proposal for circuit and certain district judges from $2,000 *per annum* to $1,800 *per annum:*

> Mr Smilie was in favor of the amendment. In Pennsylvania the Judges of the Supreme Court received only $2,000. They were men equal in legal talents to any in the Union, and had to go into every county of the State every year. It was well understood that $2,000 presented no temptation to a lawyer at the bar of Philadelphia who was in full practice. ... 10 *Annals of Congress* 902 (1801) [House debate, January 9, 1801].

During the same discussion, Mr. Bayard's sentiments were reported thusly:

> In fixing a compensation we ought to consider what sum will induce lawyers of the first talents to leave their practice. If this end were not accomplished, and men of small talents were placed on the bench, the bar would inevitably rule the bench instead of being ruled by it.
>
> Mr. B., coming from one of the smallest States in the Union, thought himself competent to forming a just opinion of the lowest allowance to the Judges that would be adequate. In the State of Delaware, a lawyer in full practice received at least four thousand dollars; which was double the salary allowed by the bill. From this view of the subject, as well as from the other views that had been taken, he considered two thousand dollars as only a moderate compensation. *Id. at* 906.

The following year, during debate concerning the merits of Supreme Court justices attending sessions of Circuit Court, Mr. Chapman of Vermont stated:

> ...If this system is to prevail, you must select your judges as you enlist soldiers. Instead of inquiring for lawyers of integrity and talents, you must look out for able-bodied men; for such as are best fitted to stand the fatigue

of constant travelling, and least liable to be affected by the inclemencies of weather. 11 *Annals of Congress* 134 (1802) [Senate debate, January 19, 1802].

QUALIFICATIONS OF APPOINTEES

In 1215, as part of the Magna Carta, King John pledged to his barons that he would "not make Justiciaries, Constables, Sheriffs, or Bailiffs, excepting of such as know the laws of the land..." This spirit seems to have continued through to the administrations of our first presidents. Concerning the qualifications of the earliest appointees to the federal bench, it is noted in Henderson, *Courts for a New Nation,* (1971):

> Washington had the opportunity to make an unusually large number of judicial appointments... . The judges to whom commissions were issued totalled thirty-three of whom twenty-eight accepted... . All were members of the bar, ... All but seven had local or state legal experience, either as judge, state prosecutor, or state attorney general. ... No statement by Washington or his contemporaries has been found to indicate that Washington in selecting district judges was motivated by anything other than a desire to obtain the best legal minds available in the several states.... *at* 30-31.
>
> President John Adam's policy in the selection of court officers and judges differed little from that of Washington, except that proper political leanings were added to the desired qualifications. *at* 90.

Even a cursory examination of Senate Committee on the Judiciary materials concerning nominees to the federal judiciary reveals that legal ability continues to be an important factor considered by Members as well as the public. Indeed, no example has been found of a federal judge appointed without previous legal experience though many have had no formal legal training, *i. e,* attendance at a law school. This was because law schools as extant today did not exist and most early lawyers trained by "reading the law" while serving an apprenticeship or clerkship in a practicing attorney's office. As recently as 1930, approximately 46% of the sitting district judges did not have law degrees. Richardson & Vines, *The Politics of Federal Courts* 74, Table 6 (1970). It was not until 1957 that, for the first time in history, the Supreme Court of the United States was composed entirely of law school graduates. Friedman & Israel, *IV The Justices of the United States Supreme Court* 3197 (1969).

CONSTITUTIONAL CONCERNS RAISED BY LAYPERSONS SERVING AS FEDERAL JUDGES

The principal constitutional objection to a person not trained in the law sitting as a federal judge is that it could be violative of the Due Process Clause of the Fifth Amendment. For a trial to be fair, a judge must have knowledge and understanding of substantive and procedural law, both gained from years of study and practice. While the Supreme Court has validated a state procedure where misdemeanor cases, with a possible sentence of imprisonment, are tried before a lay judge, this situation is only authorized if a trial *de novo* is available of right before a law-trained judge and this option is explained to the defendant. *North v. Russell,* 427 U.S. 328 (1976). A trial "anew" in one where another trial is held as though the previous proceedings on the same issue had not taken place. State statutes authorizing trial *de novo* typically involve an initial proceeding before a court not of record, *i.e.,* a low level court dealing with traffic offenses, barking dogs, small amounts of money, *etc.,* which hears relatively insignificant matters of a nature which could not be brought in federal court. Thus, there is no trial *de novo* in the federal courts.

STUDY GROUP RECOMMENDATIONS ON JUDICIAL QUALIFICATIONS

Over the years, various organizations have studied the question of qualifications for judges and have subsequently called for the professionalism of the judiciary. The considered opinion of these groups, composed of both attorneys and lay persons, is that even the most inferior court should be presided over by attorneys, *e.g.:* The president's Commission on Law Enforcement and Administration of Justice, *Task Force Report: The Courts* 36 (1967); Consensus Statement of the National Conference on the Judiciary, 59 *Journal of the American Judicature Society* 29, 30 (1971); Advisory Commission in Intergovernmental Relations, *State-Local Relations in the Criminal Justice System,* Recommendation 21 (1971); National Advisory Commission on Criminal Justice Standards and Goals, *Task Force Report: Court,* Standard 8.1 (1973); American Bar Association Commission on Standards of Judicial Administration, *Court Organization,* §1.21 (1974).

In summing up the deficiencies of a typical lay judge as they would impact upon the fair administration of justice, one respected jurist observed:

With no training in the law, no training in the process of judicial though, and no mental habit of mind acquired by constant experience in legal reasoning, it would indeed be strange if a [lay judge] did not treat each case as a unique proposition. He has no category or class into which he may place it, no analogies from which to draw to solve the new problem before him. He has no legal rules, principles or standards by which to judge the merits of the controversy to be decided. Wholly unlike the judge who is trained in the law, he has no precedents to guide him. In deciding the cause before him the lay judge is necessarily limited by his own personal experience acquired in the short span of single lifetime. He cannot call on the legal experience of the ages to assist him but is helpless to any more then apply his own personal notions of right and wrong to the case at hand. The Justice which such tribunal is capable of dispensing is but the outcropping of the experiences of a personality, often limited and warped by passion and prejudice, and at best, as variable as the personalities of the justices who comprise [the system]... . Such justice is not justice at all. It is unequal, uncertain and capricious. R. Pound, *Outlines of Lectures on Jurisprudence* 75 (3rd ed. 1963).

Chapter 4

RECESS APPOINTMENTS OF FEDERAL JUDGES

Louis Fisher

On December 27, 2000, President Bill Clinton used his recess appointment power to place Roger L. Gregory on the Fourth Circuit. The Constitution provides that such appointments "shall expire at the End of their next Session (In this case, at the end of 2001). This was the first time since President Carter that the recess appointment procedure had been used to select someone to an Article III judgeship. The appointment of Gregory raised questions about the meaning of the Recess Clause, Senate prerogatives, and the opportunity of a litigant in federal court to have a case handled by a judge with full independence.

The recess appointment power has been used in some instances for non-Article III judges. Judges on Article III, or constitutional, courts are entitled to lifetime tenures and are protected against (diminution of their salaries. Those privileges do not extend to non-Article III courts (also called Article I or legislative courts). Over the past two centuries, Article I courts have included territorial courts, legislative courts, military courts, U.S. magistrates, and, at various times, the courts of the District of Columbia. On December 10, 1997, President Clinton used his recess appointment power to place Christine Odell Cook Miller on the U.S. Court of Federal Claims, which is an Article I court because the judges have 15-year terms. Similarly, on January 19, 2001, President Clinton selected Sarah L. Wilson as a recess appointee to the same court. This report focuses on recess appointments of Article III judges.

RECESS CLAUSE

The Constitution gives the President the power to nominate, "and by and with the Advice and Consent of the Senate," appoint ambassadors, other public ministers and consuls, Justices of the Supreme Court, and "all other Officers of the United States, whose Appointments are not herein otherwise provided for, and which shall be established by Law." The President also has power "to Fill up all Vacancies that may happen during the Recess of the Senate, by granting Commissions which shall expire at the End of their next Session."[1]

The framers recognized that the Senate would not always be in session to give advice and consent to presidential nominations. To cover these periods, the President is authorized to make recess appointments that are needed to keep government operating effectively. This provision was adopted at the Constitutional Convention without a dissenting vote and with virtually no record to fix its intent and scope.[2] The power to make recess appointments is stated in general terms, with no distinctions between its application to judges or non-judges. However, there is a tension between the appointment of recess judges — serving on a temporary basis — and the general principle of judicial independence assured by lifetime tenure.

Federalist No. 67, written by Alexander Hamilton, adds little to the intent of the Recess Clause.[3] He states that the "general mode" of appointing officers of the United States required joint action by the President and the Senate, and that the Recess Clause was "nothing more than a supplement... for the purpose of establishing an auxiliary method of appointment, in cases to which the general method was inadequate." It would have been improper, he said, to oblige the Senate "to be continually in session for the appointment of officers, and as vacancies might happen *in their recess,* which it might be necessary for the public service to fill without delay, the succeeding clause is evidently intended to authorize the President, *singly,* to make temporary appointments 'during the recess of the Senate, by grating commissions which shall expire at the end of their next session.'"[4] Most of Federalist No. 67 is devoted to rejecting the claim that the president could use the Recess Clause to fill vacancies in the Senate.

---

[1] U.S. Const. art. II, § 2, cl. 3.

[2] The Records of the Federal Convention of 1787, at 540, 574, 600, 660 (New Haven: Yale University Press, 1937, Max Farrand ed.) (hereafter "Farrand"); 3 Farrand 421.

[3] The Federalist, by Alexander Hamilton, James Madison, and John Jay 436-440 (Cambridge, Mass.: Harvard University Press, 1961, Benjamin Fletcher Wright ed.).

[4] Id. at 438-39 (emphasis in original).

Vacancies that "May Happen"

Hamilton's essay raises the question of the meaning of "happen" and "recess." What does the Constitution mean when it refers to vacancies "that may happen during the Recess of the Senate"? Does happen mean "happen to take place" during the recess, as Hamilton suggested? A long list of opinions by Attorneys General has interpreted the language more broadly to mean "happen to exist" at the time of a recess, including vacancies that occur while the Senate is in session and available to give advice and consent. For example, Attorney General Wirt claimed that the second and broader meaning satisfied the reason, scope, and purpose of the Constitution, which to Wirt meant keeping offices filled.[5] Other Attorneys General have reached the same conclusion.[6] In 1880, a federal district court concurred in the position of the Attorney General in opinions issued from 1823 to 1880.[7]

"Recess" of the Senate

The word "recess" also requires interpretation. In 1901, an Attorney General opinion distinguished between the meaning of "adjournment" and "recess" in such a way as to limit *adjournment* to brief periods in the middle of a session, whereas *recess* referred to the period when Congress adjourned at the end of a session. Both words meant the suspension of legislative business, but adjournment implies "a less prolonged intermission than 'recess.'" An adjournment means a "merely temporary suspension of business from day to day, or, when exceeding three days, for such brief periods over holidays as are well recognized and established and as are agreed upon by the joint action of the two Houses." Recess refers to "the period after the final adjournment of Congress for the session, and before the next session begins." Congress "adjourns" in either case, but "[i]t is this period following the final adjournment for the session which is *the recess* during which the president has power to fill vacancies by granting commissions which shall expire at the end of the next session."[8]

---

[5] 1 Op. Att'y Gen. 631 (1823).

[6] 2 Op. Att'y Gen. 525 (1832); 4 Op. Att'y Gen. 523 (1846); 10 Op. Att'y Gen. 356 (1862); 12 Op. Att'y Gen. 32, 38 (1866); 12 Op. Att'y Gen. 455, 457 (1868); 16 Op. Att'y Gen. 522, 524 (1880); 18 Op. Att'y Gen. 29 (1884): 19 Op. Att'y Gen. 261, 262 (1889); 30 Op. Att'y Gen. 314, 315 (1914); Op. Att'y Gen. 20, 23 (1921); 41 Op. Att'y Gen. 463, 465-66 (1960).

[7] In re Farrow, 3 F. 112, 113-115 (C.C. N.D. Ga. 1880).

[8] 23 Op. Att'y Gen. 599, 601, (1901) (emphasis in original).

The opinion in 1901 said that earlier opinions by Attorneys General on the recess appointment power "relate only to appointments during the recess of the Senate between two sessions of Congress."[9] It acknowledged that if Congress "temporarily adjourned" in the middle of a session "for several months as well as several days," this practice could "seriously curtail the President's power of making recess appointments."[10] Nevertheless, the opinion continued to refer to the interval between one session and the next as "*the recess.*"[11]

An Attorney General opinion in 1921 concluded that an adjournment in the middle of a session, from August 24 to September 21, was of sufficient duration to permit recess appointments by the President. Breaking with the 1901 analysis, the Attorney General looked to the "broad and underlying purpose" of the Constitution, which is "to prohibit the President from making appointments without the advice and consent of the Senate whenever that body is in session so that its advice and consent can be obtained." As to whether the Senate "has adjourned or recessed, the real question, as I view it, is whether in a *practical* sense the Senate is in session so that its advice and consent can be obtained. To give the 'recess' a technical and not a practical construction, is to disregard substance for form."[12]

If a President could make recess appointments during an intrasession adjournment from August 24 to September 21, "does it not necessarily follow that the power exists if an adjournment for only 2 instead of 28 days is taken? I unhesitatingly answer this by saying no."[13] The term "recess" required "a practical construction." When the Senate adjourns for two days, it remains in session. "Nor do I think an adjournment for 5 or even 10 days can be said to constitute the recess intended by the Constitution."[14] In referring to a Senate report written in 1905, the opinion said that the "essential inquiry" consists of these questions: "Is the adjournment of such duration that the members of the Senate owe no duty of attendance? Is its chamber empty? Is the Senate absent so that it can not receive communications from the President or participate as a body in making appointments?"[15]

Subsequent opinions from the Attorney General agreed that significant interruptions in the middle of a session could justify the President's use of the recess appointment power. According to an opinion in 1960, a temporary recess of

[9] Id. at 602.
[10] Id. at 603.
[11] Id. at 604 (emphasis in original).
[12] 33 Op. Att'y Gen. 20, 21-22 (1921) (emphasis in original).
[13] Id. at 24.
[14] Id. at 25.
[15] Id.

the Senate, "protracted enough to prevent that body from reforming its functions of advising and consenting to executive nominations," permits the President to make recess appointments.[16] Following this interpretation, the Senate's adjournment from July 3 to August 8 in 1960 constituted a "Recess of the Senate."[17]

Opinions by Attorneys General have concluded that short adjournments "for 5 or even 10 days" do not "constitute the recess intended by the Constitution."[18] In 1979, an opinion by the Office of Legal Counsel in the Justice Department held that a recess from August 2 until September 4, 1979, would be of sufficient length to entitle the President to make recess appointments.[19] A Justice Department brief in 1993 suggested that recess appointments might be justified for recesses in excess of three days, but the litigation that prompted this statement was not decided on that ground.[20]

Comptroller General Rulings

The Comptroller General of the General Accounting Office has also offered interpretations of the President's power to make recess appointments. In 1948, the Comptroller General received a letter from the Director of the Administration Office of the U.S. Courts, regarding the right of payment to four U.S. judges appointed on a recess basis after the senate adjourned June 20, 1948, to return on December 31, 1948. The Comptroller General cited with approval an earlier Attorney General opinion, which had upheld the use of the President's recess appointment power during an adjournment from August 24 to September 21, 1921.[21] However, the Comptroller General also ruled that one of the judges was not entitled to payment of salary because of a statutory provision that prohibited payment of salary to an individual who had received a recess appointment during a previous recess of the Senate.[22]

---

16 41 Op. Att'y Gen. 463, 466 (1960).
17 Id.
18 33 Op. Att'y Gen. 20, 25 (1921).
19 3 Op. Off. Legal Counsel 314 (1979).
20 Memorandum of Points and Authorities in Support of Defendant's Opposition to Plaintiffs' Motion for Partial Summary Judgment, at 24-26, *Mackie v. Clinton*, Civ. Action No. 93-0032-LFO (D.D.C.).
21 28 Comp. Gen. 30, 34-37 (1948).
22 Id. at 37-38.

FUNDING LIMITATIONS

The broad reading of the Recess Clause by Attorneys General prompted Congress to invoke its power of the purse to limit presidential actions. After Attorneys General had handed down a number of opinions on the power to make recess appointments, Senator William Fessenden remarked in 1836: "It may not be in our power to prevent the [recess] appointment, but it is in our power to prevent the payment; and when payment is prevented, I think that will probably put an end to the habit of making such appointments."[23]

Fessenden made his comment after the Senate had asked its Judiciary Committee to explore this question: Did the practice of appointing officers to fill vacancies that existed *prior* to a recess, while the Senate was in session, conflict with the Constitution? The committee rejected Attorney General Wirt's position that a recess appointee may fill a vacancy that occurs during a session. To the committee, interpreting the constitutional language "may happen during the Recess of the Senate" to include what happened before the recess represented "a perversion of language." Such reasoning, said the committee, titled political power toward the President and placed undue emphasis on the filling of a vacancy at the expense of Senate prerogatives. Of equal importance to filling vacancies was the need to protect the Senate's opportunity to pass judgement on the qualification of an officeholder. Unless Congress placed some constraint on the President's power to make recess appointments, an "ambitious, corrupt, or tyrannical executive" could nullify the Senate's constitutional function.[24]

Statutory Language in 1863

Congress passed legislation in 1863 to prohibit the use of funds to pay the salary of anyone appointed during a Senate recess to fill a vacancy that existed "while the Senate was in session and is by law required to be filled by and with the advice and consent of the Senate, until such appointee shall have been confirmed by the Senate."[25] Because of this funding restriction, an officer might have to serve without pay (relying on savings or loans) until the Senate consented to the nomination.

---

[23] Cong Globe, 37th Cong., 3rd sess.565 (1863).
[24] S. Rept. No. 80, 37th Cong., 3rd sess. 5-6 (1863).
[25] 12 Stat. 646 (1863).

That situation arose during the administration of Woodrow Wilson. George Rublee, nominated to the Federal Trade Commission in March 1915, served for more than a year as a recess appointee. After the Senate voted to reject him, he continued to serve the balance of his recess commission until September 1916, when Congress adjourned. Because of the 1836 legislation, Rublee was not entitled to any remuneration Congress had to pass a special appropriation to pay his salary for fourteen months: from the date his service began to the date the Senate rejected him.[26]

Revisions in 1940

In 1940, Congress revised the 1863 law to make it less burdensome on officeholders. Congress changed the law to allow for three exceptions in what is now 5 U.S.C. § 5503. As a general rule, payment may not be made to an individual appointed during a Senate recess to fill an existing office of the vacancy existed while the Senate was in session and was by law required to be filled with Senate advice and consent, until the appointee has confirmed by the Senate.

However, there are three exceptions. First, payments may be made if a vacancy arises within 30 days before the end of the session of the Senate. Given the shortness of time, nominations submitted during that period would be unlikely to gain the Senate's approval. Second, payments may be made if, at the end of the session, a nomination for the office is pending before the Senate (other than for someone appointed during a preceding recess). This provision protects the Senate from successive recess appointees, and it protects nominees whose names go forward in timely manner. Third, payments may be made if a nomination is rejected by the Senate within 30 days before the end of the session and individual (other than the one rejected) receives a recess appointment. This exception takes care of possible rejections on the eve of a recess. Moreover, the 1940 statute contains an important limitation: A nomination to fill a vacancy referred to in the three exceptions must be submitted to the Senate not later than 40 days after the Senate's next session begins.[27] "Next session" has been interpreted in a nontechnical way to mean the return of the Senate from its recess, not the next session of a Congress.[28]

---

[26] 39 Stat. 801 (1916).
[27] 54 Stat. 751 (1950); 5 U.S.C. § 5503 (1994).
[28] 41 Op. Att'y Gen. 463, 477 (1960).

Dispute in 2001

The application of § 5503 to Article I judges was raised in 2001, after President Clinton made a recess appointment of Sarah L. Wilson to the U.S. Court of Federal Claims. President Clinton nominated her after the 107th Congress convened on January 3, 2001.[29] The Senate then recessed from January 8 to January 20. She was given a recess appointment on January 19 but her nomination was not resubmitted to the Senate, as required under § 5503(b).

Senator Strom Thurmond wrote to the Administrative Office of the U.S. Courts on May 9, stating his belief that Wilson's salary should be suspended because her appointment violated § 5503. He suggested that the Administrative office request an opinion on the issue from the Office of Personnel Management or the General Accounting Office.[30] William R. Burchill, Jr., Associate Director and General Counsel of the Administrative Office, replied on May 24 that in the opinion of the Administrative Office it was appropriate to pay Judge Wilson's salary and there was no need to seek any outside confirmation of this understanding. Burchill said that Wilson feel within the exception set forth in subsection (a) (2) of § 5503, which states that the salary cutoff shall not apply if, at the end of a session, "a nomination for the office, other than the nomination of an individual appointed during the preceding recess of the Senate, was pending before the Senate for its advice and consent. " Wilson's nomination was pending before the Senate when it recessed on January 8.

Burchill agreed that § 5503(b) terminates the entitlement of a recess appointee to pay. However, he said that analyses by the Office of Legal Counsel left it unsettled as to whether the language "next session" in § 5503(b) refers to a post–recess reconvening of the same Congress or the beginning of the session of a Congress that succeeds the adjournment sine die of the current one.[31]

Annual Limitations

In addition to the funding restrictions in § 5503, funding limitations have been included in the annual Treasury-Postal Service appropriations bill. For example, this language appeared in 2000: "No part of any appropriation for the

[29] 37 Weekly Comp. Pres. Doc. 105 (2001).

[30] Letter from Senator Strom Thurmond to the Honorable Leonidas Ralph Mecham, Director, Administrative Office of the U.S. Courts, May 9, 2001.

[31] Letter from William R. Buchill, Jr., Associate Director and General Counsel of the Administrative Office of the U.S. Courts to Senator Strom Thurmond, May 24, 2001, at 2.

current fiscal year contained in this or any other Act shall be paid to any person for the filling of any position for which he or she has been nominated after the Senate has voted not to approve the nomination of said person."[32]

"HOLDOVER" PROVISIONS

The scope of the recess appointment power can be complicated by the presence of "holdover" clauses in federal statutes. These clauses do not concern the appointment of federal judges, but they have been extensively litigated and help in defining the meaning and application of the Recess Clause. These cases emphasize how Congress, by enacting legislation, can specify when a vacancy exists and expand or limit the President's opportunity to make a recess appointment.

The *Staebler* Case

As an example of a holdover clause, a member of the Federal Election Commission may serve after the expiration of that member's term "until his successor has taken office as a member of the Commission." This type of statutory provision has been litigated because it is unclear how the successor takes office: by Senate confirmation (required for new members) or as a recess appointee. According to the FEC statute, any vacancy in the membership of the commission "shall be filled in the same manner as in the case of the original appointment" (presumably by Senate confirmation). However, on October 25, 1978, President Carter made John McGarry a recess appointee to the seat held by Neil Staebler, who was serving in a holdover capacity. Staebler refused to leave office, arguing that McGarry had not been confirmed by the Senate and therefore no vacancy existed for Carter to fill.

A federal district judge, deciding against Staebler, pointed to some difficulties with the statute. If a vacancy existed only at the point of confirmation for a successor, this might place an unmanageable task on the President. How could he recruit someone for the office and submit a nomination if, in theory, no vacancy existed? The court also concluded that such a result would disrupt the statutory design of staggered, six-year terms for the six commissioners. Following Staebler's interpretation, the statutory dates for these terms might shift to take

[32] 114 Stat. 2763A-157, § 609 (2000).

account of holdovers, creating a "baggage of peculiar practical difficulties."[33] The court could find no clear evidence that Congress had tried to restrict the President's power to make recess appointments.[34] If the Senate wanted to protect its right to advise and consent, it could have rejected McGarry's nomination when Carter first sent it up on September 27, 1977, and again on April 10, 1978. It was only after two years of Senate inaction that Carter made the recess appointment.[35] On appeal, the D.C. Circuit dismissed the case as moot, remanding it to the district court.

Controversies over holdover positions turn on the particular language that Congress enacts. The power to make recess appointments has been a major issue in the life of the Legal Services Corporation (LSC). Through the use of holdover provisions and recess appointments, Presidents Reagan and Bush were able to largely circumvent the Senate's power of confirmation. Several recent court decisions explore the President's power to make recess appointments to the LSC and to other agencies.[36] These decisions analyzed statutory language, such as the length of time the person could remain on holdover status, and whether the holdover "shall" or "may continue to serve in office. Thus, the scope of the recess appointment power in these areas depends on the particular language that Congress places in a statute.

POLITICAL ACCOMMODATIONS

Confrontations over recess appointments in the 1980s and 1990s led to political agreement between the executive and legislative branches. Although Presidents claimed full constitutional authority to exercise the Recess Clause, they recognized that excessive use of this power could trigger credible threats from Senators to place a hold on all nominations until the White House agreed to an acceptable compromise that satisfied the institutional prerogatives of both branches.

---

33 *Staebler v. Carter*, 464 F. Supp. 585, 589 (D.D.C. 1979).

34 Id. at 592.

35 Id. at 601. For the Senate's record on McGarry, see id. at 587.

36 *Swan v. Clinton*, 100 F.3d 973 (D.C. Cir. 1996); *Wilkinson v. Legal Services Corp.*, 865 F. Supp. 891 (D.D.C. 1994), reversed on other grounds, *Wilkinson v. Legal Services Corp.*, 80 F. 3d 535 (D.C. Cir. 1996); *Mackie v. Clinton*, 827 F. Supp. 56 (D.D.C. 1993); *McCalpin v. Durant*, 766 F. 2d 535 (D.C. Cir. 1985); *McCalpin v. Dana*, No. 85-542 (D.D.C. 1982). See "An LSC Dispute May Take Power from President," National Law Journal, February 19, 1996, at A1.

Nomination of Martha Seger

On May 31, 1984, President Reagan nominated Martha R. Seger to be a member of the Board of Governors of the Federal Reserve System.[37] The Senate Banking Committee had held four days of hearings and approved her nomination by the close vote of 10 to 8. A Spirited floor debate was expected, but that was foreclosed when Reagan gave her a recess appointment on July 2 after Congress took a three-week break for the Fourth of July holiday (from June 29 to July 23).[38] Senator William Proxmire, chairman of the Banking Committee, accused Reagan of abusing his recess appointment powers and promised to devise remedies that would restrict the President's authority.[39] Lawmakers also objected to other recess appointments made by Reagan.[40]

On August 8, Senator Max Baucus offered an amendment to a supplemental appropriations bills, calling on President Reagan to withdraw the recess appointment for Seger. The Senate voted 53-43 to table the amendment.[41] A day later, Senate Minority Leader Robert C. Byrd introduced a Senate resolution (S.Res. 430), stating that it was the sense of the Senate that the power to make recess appointments should be confined to situations in which the Senate has formally terminated a session or in which the Senate will be in recess for longer than 30 days.[42] That resolution was never put to a vote, but a year later the Senate passed a different resolution offered by Senator Proxmire (S.Res. 149), expressing the sense of the Senate that recess appointments should not be made to the Federal Reserve Board except under unusual circumstances, and only for the purpose of fulfilling "a demonstrable and urgent need" in the administration of the board's activities. The Senate also agreed to consider nominations to the board in an expeditious manner. The resolution was agreed to by voice vote.[43]

On June 13, 1985, the Senate confirmed Seger by voice vote for a term expiring in 1998. On this occasion the Senate Banking Committee voted 11-4 for her confirmation.[44] Although there was controversy over her recess appointment, there was never a question of using a funding restriction to deny appropriated

---

[37] Public Papers of the Presidents, 1984, II, at 777.

[38] Id. at 1915.

[39] "Proxmire: Seger Appointment Cut Constitutional Corners," *Washington Post*, July 6, 1984, at D3.

[40] Reagan's Recess Hirings Elicit Resentment," *Washington Post*, July 11, 1984, at A17; "Reagan's Recess Appointments Rankle Hill," *Washington Post*, July 14, 1984, at 1968.

[41] 130 Cong. Rec. 22767-82 (1984).

[42] Id. at 23234-36, 23341.

[43] 131 Cong. Rec. 17622-24, 17679 (1985).

[44] 1985 CQ Almanac 420.

funds for her salary. The Federal Reserve relies on nonappropriated funds to support its operations.

A separate Byrd resolution (S. Res. 213), Which the Senate did not act on, stated that the recess appointment power should be confined to a formal termination of a session of the Senate or a recess "protracted enough to prevent it from discharging its constitutional function of advising and consenting to executive nominations." Moreover, it stated that since Presidents and departmental heads were authorized by the Vacancies Act at that time to make temporary appointments for at least 30 days, "no recess appointment should be made when the Senate stands adjourned or recessed within a session for a period of less than thirty days." Finally, the resolution stated that no recess appointment should be made of any person to any office (1) if the person has previously, during the same presidential term, been nominated for appointment to the office, and (2) the Senate has voted not to give its advice and consent to such appointment, or the appropriate committee of the Senate has voted not to report the nomination to the Senate.[45]

Agreement with Senator Byrd

On July 30, 1985, when the Senate was about to recess for the August break, Senator Byrd wrote to President Reagan, stating that the recess should not be considered "the kind of extended recess" contemplated for recess appointments. A broader interpretation, he said, could be seen as "a deliberate effort to circumvent the Constitutional responsibility of he Senate to advise and consent to such appointments."[46] When President Reagan continued to use his recess appointment power broadly, Byrd responded late in 1985 by holding up action on presidential nominations.[47] Senate Majority Leader Bob Dole spoke on September 30 about Byrd's "real concern" about recess appointments and hoped to set up a meeting with the Administration "to allay some of the concerns the distinguished minority leader has."[48] On October 8, the White House announced that President Reagan was "deeply displeased" that Byrd had held up 70 appointments "touching

[45] Id. at 22419, 22496-97.

[46] Id. at 22498.

[47] "Recess Appointments Raise Senator's Anger," *Washington Post*, September 26, 1985, at A23; Public Papers of the Presidents, 1985 (II), at 1209; "White House Asks End of Appointee 'Backlog,'" *Washington Post*, October 9, 1985, at A17.

[48] 131 Cong. Rec. 25303 (1985).

virtually every area of the executive branch," including executive officials and federal judges.[49]

On October 10, a meeting was held in Senator Byrd's office to discuss the problem of recess appointments. In attendance were Senators Dole, Daniel Inouye, Strom Thurmond, and Howard Metzenbaum, plus two officials from the White House, Max Friedersdorf and Fred Fielding. It was agreed that the White House would give notice to the majority and minority leaders prior to a recess, and that the notice would be enough in advance to give the leaders an opportunity to comment on potential recess appointments.[50]

George Mitchell Understanding

On August 4, 1989, Senate Majority Leader George Mitchell warned President George Bush not to give a recess appointment to William Lucas, who had been rejected by the Senate Judiciary Committee to head the Civil Rights Division in the Justice Department. Mitchell argued that the recess appointment power should not be used to sidestep the Senate, and that making a recess appointment of a nominee "who was considered and rejected by the relevant Senate committee… would be a very unwise course of action."[51] Lucas did not receive the recess appointment. Instead, Bush named him to be director of the Justice Department's Office of Liaison services, a position that did not require Senate confirmation.[52]

In November 1989, White House Chief of Staff John Sununu suggested that unless the Senate moved more quickly on nominations, President Bush might resort to recess appointments.[53] In a floor statement, Mitchell reiterated the understanding that Senator Byrd had developed on procedures for recess appointments, especially the practice of Presidents notifying party leaders in advance of recess appointments.[54] In 1993, in response to a recess appointment made by President Bush less than two weeks before leaving office, Senator Mitchell placed in the *Congressional Record* an analysis of the recess appointment power prepared by the Senate Legal Counsel. It had been prepared as

[49] Public Papers of the Presidents, 1985, II, at 1209; "White House Asks End to Appointee 'Backlog,'" *Washington Post*, October 9, 1985, at A17.

[50] 131 Cong. Rec. 27312-13, 27686-87 (1985).

[51] "Mitchell Oppose Recess Appointment," *Washington Post*, August 5, 1989, at A5.

[52] 1989 CQ Almanac 31.

[53] "Senate Pressed on Nominees," *Washington Post*, November 11, 1989, at A25.

[54] 135 Cong. Rec. 28390, 31445-46 (1989); "Mitchell Cautions On Appointments," *Washington Post*, November 15, 1989, at A19.

an amicus brief, to present the Senate's position in a pending recess appointment case, but failed to receive the necessary bipartisan support. The analysis reviewed earlier understandings that the recess appointment power would be utilized "only, and rarely, during substantial intrasession breaks." However, that understanding had now been replaced by the executive branch's claim that "there is no lower time limit" in making recess appointments, a position that "threatens to produce a high level of uncertainty, with regard to appointments, into the relationship between the branches."[55]

Guidelines under Clinton

When the Senate recessed on August 2, 1996, to return on September 3, there was speculation about who President Clinton might appoint on a recess basis. It was considered unlikely that he would make recess appointments of six pending names for federal judgeships: Merrick Garland for the D.C. Circuit, Arthur Gajarsa for the Federal Circuit, William A. Fletcher for the Ninth Circuit, Eric Clay for the Sixth Circuit, and Margaret M. Morrow and Susan McIlway for district court seats. Senate objections would be strong, placing other nominations in jeopardy. Also, the candidates for these federal positions, "especially out-of-towners with families to move, often say would prefer waiting around for confirmation rather than risk losing the new appointment after little more than a year on the job."[56]

On June 4, President Clinton issued a recess appointment to James C. Hormel to be ambassador to Luxembourg. The Senate was in recess from May 27 to June 7. When the Senate returned, Senator James Inhofe announced: "I am going to do the same thing Senator Byrd did back in 1985: I am putting holds on every single Presidential nomination."[57] Inhofe charged that Clinton treated the Senate confirmation process "as little more than a nuisance which he can circumvent whenever he wants to impose his will on the country."[58] Infore said he would continue to block nominations until Clinton agreed to make them only if Congress was notified in advance and they were "absolutely necessary."[59]

[55] 139 Cong. Rec. 15267 (1993). See "Recess Appointments: A Disputed Matter of Timing," *Washington Post*, July 19, 1993, at A13.

[56] "The Recess Appointment Game," *Washington Post*, August 12, 1996, at A11.

[57] 145 Cong. Rec. S6654 (daily ed. June 8, 1999).

[58] "Choice of Hormel Spurs Vow to Block Nominees," *Washington Post*, June 9, 1999, at A23.

[59] "In Protest of Clinton Action, Senator Blocks Nominations," *New York Times*, June 9, 1999, at A2.

President Clinton has followed the practice of notifying Senate leaders before a recess when he intended to make a recess appointment. In the case of Hormel, however, he did not notify the leaders until June 3, the night before he made the appointment. By that time the Senate had already been in recess for a week.[60] In his response to the Inhofe threat, Clinton wrote to Senator Lott on June 15, stating that his Administration "has made it a practice to notify Senate leaders in advance of our intentions in this regard, and this precedent will continue to be observed."[61] With that agreement in place, Inhofe dropped his threat to block nominations.[62]

The issue flared up again on November 17, 1999, when Senator Inhofe challenged what he considered to be an improper use of the recess appointment power. It was his position that recess appointments "can only be made in the event the vacancy occurs during the recess."[63] A more expansive reading, he said, would magnify executive power at the expense of the Senate prerogative of advice and consent. He reviewed the understanding that Senator Byrd and President Reagan had reached in 1985. Prior to any recess break, the White House would inform the Majority Leader and the Minority Leader of any recess appointment that might be contemplated during the recess. The advance notice would be sufficiently early to allow the leadership on both sides to take action to fill "whatever vacancies that might be imperative during such a break."[64]

President Clinton had agreed to that procedure in his June 15, 1999, letter to Senator Lott, in which he said "I share your opinion that the understanding reached in 1985 between President Reagan and Senator Byrd cited in your letter remains a fair and constructive framework, which my Administration will follow."[65] If the Administration violated the spirit of the agreement, Inhofe and 15 other Senators advised Clinton by letter that they would place holds on "all judicial nominees."[66]

Senator Inhofe read into the *Congressional Record* the names of 13 people submitted by the White House for appointment.[67] The White House–Senate agreement provided a framework but was not strictly adhered to. Some recess

---

[60] "Clinton Vow to Congress Ends a Threat to His Nominations," *New York Times*, June 17, 1999, at A22.

[61] Id.

[62] "Inhofe Ends Threat to Clinton Nominees," *Washington Post*, June 17, 1999, at A17.

[63] 145 Cong. Rec. S14665 (daily ed. November 17, 1999).

[64] Id.

[65] Id. at S14666.

[66] Id. The Senators signing the letter included Jesse Helms, Wayne Allard, Michael Crapo, Michael B. Enzi, Bob Smith, George Voinovich, Pete B. Dominici, James M. Inhofe, Phil Gramm, Mitch McConnell, Craig Thomas, Rod Grams, Tim Hutchinson, Conrad Burns, Chuck Grassley, and Richard Shelby.

[67] Id. at S15060 (daily ed. November 19, 1999).

appointments were made of names not on the list, and Senator Inhofe was unable to place a total hold on all judicial nominees.[68] On February 11, 2000, the Senate approved Thomas L. Ambro for the Third Circuit and Joel A. Pisano for a district judgeship.[69]

RECESS APPOINTMENTS OF ARTICLE III JUDGES

In 1789, President George Washington made three recess appointments to the federal district courts.[70] From 1789 to 1799, the recess appointment power was used to appoint nine other individuals to federal courts.[71] All were later confirmed by the Senate, except for John Rutledge, who Washington had made Chief Justice under a recess appointment.

John Rutledge

In 1975, John Jay resigned his position as Chief Justice to assume the office of Governor of New York. On July 1, President Washington wrote to John Rutledge of South Carolina, stating that his commission as Chief Justice would take effect on that day as a recess appointee.[72] Rutledge had served as Associate Justice of the U.S. Supreme Court from 1789 to 1791, but resigned that position to become Chief Justice of the South Carolina Court of Common Pleas.

After having named Chief Justice as a recess appointee, Rutledge gave an intemperate speech on July 16, 1795, bitterly attacking the Jay Treaty. He called it

---

[68] "Recess appointee wasn't on list," *Washington Times*, December 22, 1999, at A1; "Senator Vows to Stall Action on Judgeships," *New York Times*, December 21, 1999, at A22; 146 Cong. Rec. S582-584 (daily ed. February 10, 2000): CRS Report RL30821, "Recess Appointments Made by President Clinton," By Rogelio Garcia (January 26, 2001).

[69] 146 Cong. Rec. S584-89 (February 10, 2000); "Lott Overrides 'Holds': Two Judges Confirmed," *Washington Post*, February 11, 2000, at A4.

[70] 30 The Writing of George Washington 457-58, 473, 485 n. 75. (Washington, D.C.: Government Printing Office, 1940).

[71] Robert Morris, recess appointment of August 28, 1790; William Lewis, July 14, 1791; Thomas Johnson, August 5, 1791; Samuel Hitchcock, September 3, 1793; John Rutledge, July 1, 1795; Joseph Clay, Jr., September 16, 1796; Benjamin Bourne, October 13, 1796; Bushrod Washington, September 29, 1798; James Winchester, October 1, 1799 (Second Supplemental Brief for the United States, *United States v. Woodley*, No. 82-1028, Ninth Circuit, 1983, at A1-A25).

[72] 34 The Writings of George Washington 225. The Temporary commission is reprinted in 1 Documentary History of the Supreme Court of the United States, 1789-1800, at 96 (New York: Columbia University Press, 1985, Maeva Marcus & James R. Perry, eds.).

a surrender of American privileges and a "prostitution of the dearest rights of free men." Calling provisions in the treaty the "grossest absurdities" and "ridiculous and inadmissible," he said it would be better for President Washington to die, much as he loved him, than sign the treaty.[73] The speech prompted reports that Rutledge was insane and "daily sinking into debility of mind and body."[74]

On December 10, 1795, President Washington nominated Rutledge to a full life term as Chief Justice. The Senate defeated the nomination five days later, voting 10 to 14.[75] The debate on the nomination is not included in the *Annals of Congress* or the *Senate Executive Journal.* on December 26, Rutledge attempted to drown himself by jumping off a wharf into Charleston Bay.[76] Two days later he wrote to President Washington, resigning his commission as a recess appointee to the position of Chief Justice. He said he was "convinced by Experience, that it requires a Constitution less broken than mine, to discharge with Punctuality & Satisfaction, the Duties of so important an Office."[77]

Presidents continued to make recess appointments for federal judges. In 1983, as an appendix to a brief filed in the case of *United States v. Woodley,* the Justice Department prepared a list of 309 individuals who had received recess appointments to Article III courts.[78]

Eisenhower's Appointments

President Dwight D. Eisenhower placed three men on the Supreme Court after recesses by the Senate: Earl Warren, William J. Brennan, Jr., and Potter Stewart. Warren was appointed on a recess basis on October 2, 1953, Brennan on October 15, 1956, and Stewart on October 14, 1958. All three joined the Court and participated in decisions before the Senate had an opportunity to review their credentials. In each case the Senate later gave its advice and consent, but the experience convinced a number of Senators that the procedure was defective for the Senate as well as for the Court.

An article in the *Stanford Law Review* in 1957 reviewed previous recess appointments to the Supreme Court. Although nine such appointments occurred

---

[73] Leon Friedman, "John Rutledge," in 1 The Justices of the United States Supreme Court, 1789-1969, at 45 (New York: Chelsea House Publishers, 1969).

[74] Id. at 46.

[75] 1 Journal of the Executive proceedings of the Senate 195-96.

[76] Friedman, "John Rutledge," at 48.

[77] 1 Documentary History of the Supreme Court 100.

[78] Second Supplemental Brief for the United States, *United States v. Woodley*, No. 82-1028. Ninth Circuit, at A1-A25.

from 1791 to 1862, 91 years elapsed before the recess appointment of Earl Warren. Moreover, of he nine appointments, only two nominees (John Rutledge in 1795 and Benjamin Curtis in 1851) sat on the Court and participated in decisions before being nominated for a life term.[79] The article discussed a number of problems with recess appointments to the federal courts, including the need for a judge to participate and decide cases while having "one eye over his shoulder on Congress," possibly depriving the litigants of a fair hearing.[80]

Member of the House were also concerned about placing individuals on the courts on a recess basis. In January 1959, the House Committee on the Judiciary released a 40-page report entitled "Recess Appointments of Federal Judges." In transmitting the report, committee chairmen Emanuel Celler said that the purpose of lifetime appointments "is to secure independence of mind to our judges." If someone is placed on the court with a recess appointment, that person might "measure his decisions" against the knowledge that the Senate Judiciary Committee will later question those rulings. Moreover, it could be argued that the Constitution "guarantees litigants a trial before lifetime judges."[81]

One May 5, 1959, the Senate confirmed Potter Steward as a Justice of the Supreme Court by the vote of 70 to 17.[82] During the debate, Senator Philip Hart expressed his concern about passing judgement on a judicial nominee who has already been sitting as a recess appointee. As a member of the Senate Committee on the Judiciary with the responsibility for evaluating judicial nominees, he said that the practice of making interim appointments to the Court and having the appointee take his place on the Court "is one which should cease."[83]

Senate Resolution in 1960

In 1960, Senator Hart introduced S.Ress. 334 to discourage Presidents from using recess appointments for Justices of the Supreme Court. The resolution stated that it was the sense of the Senate that this type of recess appointment "is not wholly consistent with the best interests of the Supreme Court, the nominee who may be involved, the litigants before the Court, nor indeed the people of the United States." Such appointments should be avoided "except under unusual and

[79] "Recess Appointments to the Supreme Court – Constitutional But Unwise?," 10 Stan. L. Rev. 124, 125, 131 (1957).

[80] Id. at 144.

[81] "Recess Appointments of Federal Judges," House Committee on the Judiciary, 86th Cong., 1st sess. iii (Comm. Print, January 1959).

[82] 105 Cong. Rec. 7472 (1959).

[83] Id. at 7467.

urgent circumstances" and, in all such cases, the appointee should not take his seat on the Court until the Senate had given its advice and consent.[84]

As reported by the Senate Committee on the Judiciary, the resolution spoke about institutional interests, such as the "solemn constitutional tasks" of the Senate giving or withholding advice and consent with respect to nominations made to the Supreme court, and doing so, "if possible, in an atmosphere free from pressures inimincal to due deliberations." Nominations for the Court "should be considered only in the light of the qualifications the person brings to the threshold of the office." Although previous Presidents had made recess appointments to the Court, "which actions were unquestionably taken in good faith and with a desire to promote the public interest," those appointments were not made with "a full appreciation of the difficulties thereby caused the members of this body." Finally, there is "inevitably public speculation" about the independence of a Justice serving on a recess basis, forced to sit in judgment on cases prior to Senate confirmation. Such speculation, "however ill founded, is distressing to the Court, to the Justice, to the litigants, an to the Senate of the United States."[85]

As a Senate resolution, Hart's proposal could have no legally binding effect, but it was intended to express the position of the Senate and to guide executive actions. Senator Hart referred to the difficulty under which the Senate operated when asked to pass upon the nomination of someone who had already taken a seat as a Justice of the Supreme Court: "it operates to a very great disadvantage upon the Members of the Senate, and I suggest that if this should develop as a traditional practice, as what should be done always, rather than under unusual circumstances, it would adversely affect the Court."[86]

Jefferson B. Fordham, dean of the University of Pennsylvania Law School, remarked that a recess appointee "is serving under the overhang of Senate consideration of a nomination, which is not in harmony with the constitutional policy of judicial Independence."[87] Senator Hart added that disappointed litigants might wonder whether the outcome of their case had been influenced by a judge's recess status. Judicial independence, in his view, could be affected by several factors:

> Either to take a position during his period of probation which would please the President who had appointed him and who could withdraw his name; or to please the Senate, which sooner or later, would either approve or

[84] 106 Cong. Rec. 12761 (1960).
[85] S. Rept. No. 1893, 86th Cong., 2nd sess. 1-2 (1960).
[86] 106 Cong. Rec. 18131 (1960).
[87] Id. at 18132.

> disapprove; or, at the other extreme, conscious of the fact that there would be public scrutiny and interpretation of his action in light of whether he was bending to the Senate or to the President, he could rear back and bend the other way in order to prove that he was subservient to neither branch.[88]

Opponents of the resolution argued that he President needs to make recess appointments because of the Court's heavy workload.[89] They regarded the filling of vacancies on the Court during recesses as a constitutional power lodged in the President, and felt the Senate should not attempt to meddle with it.[90] It was noted that the power of the Senate is limited to the time after a Justice is nominated, not before.[91] Some Senators objected that the resolution's language was phrased in ambiguous fashion.[92] Finally, it was objected that the resolution had never been referred to the Justice Department of the Judicial Conference for comment, nor had there been any hearing on the resolution.[93] The resolution, including the preamble, reads as follows:

> Whereas one of the solemn constitutional tasks enjoined upon the Senate is to give or withhold its advice and consent with respect to nominations made to the Supreme Court of the United States, doing so, if possible, in an atmosphere free from pressures inimical to due deliberation: and
>
> Whereas the nomination of a person to the office of Justice of the Supreme Court should be considered only in the light of the qualifications the person brings to threshold of the office; and
>
> Whereas Presidents of the United States have from time to time made recess appointments to the Supreme Court, which actions were unquestionably taken in good faith and with a desire to promote the public interest, but without a full appreciation of the difficulties thereby caused the Members of this body; and
>
> Whereas there is inevitably public speculation on the independence of a Justice serving by recess appointment who sits in judgement upon cases prior to his confirmation by this body, which speculation, however ill founded, is distressing to the Court, to the Justice, to the litigants, and to the Senate of the United States: Now, therefore be it
>
> *Resolved,* That it is the sense of the Senate that the making of recess appointments to the Supreme Court of the United States may not be wholly consistent with the best interests of the Supreme Court, the nominee who may be involved, the litigants before the Court, nor indeed the people of the

[88] Id. at 18134.
[89] Id. at 18133 (Senator Hruska).
[90] Id. at 18134 (Senator Wiley).
[91] Id. at 18135 (Senator Wiley).
[92] Id.
[93] Id. at 18137 (Senator Hruska).

United States, and that such appointments, therefore, should not be made except under unusual circumstances and for the purpose of preventing or ending a demonstrable breakdown in the administration of the Court's business.

The Senate passed the resolution 48 to 37, voting largely along party lines.[94] Democrats supported it 48-4, with Republicans opposed 33 to 0. The four Democrats voting against the resolution were Edmund Muskie of Maine, Frank Lausche of Ohio, John Pastore of Rhode Island, and Albert Gore of Tennessee.[95]

LITIGATION

The constitutionality of recess appointments to the federal bench has been litigated in two cases in federal circuit courts. The Supreme Court has not ruled on the issue. When the two cases reached the Court for review, the Court denied certiorari. One case resulted from an appointment by President Dwight D. Eisenhower in 1955. The other case involved an appointment by President Jimmy Carter in 1980.

The *Allocco* Case

On July 31, 1955, Judge Samuel H. Kaufman retired as U.S. district judge for the Southern District of New York. On August 17, President Eisenhower issued a recess appointment to John M. Cashin to fill the vacancy left by Kaufman. Cashin took the oath of office for the recess appointment on September 15. Dominic Allocco was tried before Judge Cashin, found guilty by a jury on October 20, and sentenced to 10 years imprisonment. After the Senate reconvened in January 1956, Cashin was confirmed by the Senate and commissioned as a judge with life tenure. He took the oath of office for the commission on March 9, 1956.

Allocco argued that his sentence should be set aside because Judge Cashin was not constitutionally empowered to preside over the trial. He maintained that (1) the President has no power to appoint "temporary" judges, (2) if the President can make interim appointments of judges, they may not preside over criminal

---

[94] Id. at 18145.
[95] 1960 CQ Almanac, at 517.

trials, and (3) the President has no power to fill vacancies in the judiciary that arise when the Senate is in session.[96]

The Second Circuit ruled that Judge Cashin was constitutionally empowered to preside over the trial. It noted the Constitution expressly gives the President power to fill up "all" vacancies and that there are no exceptions for judges, which the petitioner wanted the court to find.[97] Since Article II permits the President to make recess appointments for judges, "it necessarily follows that such judicial officers may exercise the power granted to Article III courts," including criminal trials.[98] As to the charge that Presidents may not use the recess appointment power to fill vacancies that arise while the Senate is in session, the court held that this interpretation "would create Executive paralysis and do violence to the orderly functioning of our complex government."[99] The one law review article written in response to this decision was critical of the court's analysis.[100]

The *Woodley* Case

President Carter nominated Walter Heen for a district judgeship in Hawaii on February 28, 1980. On September 25, the Senate Judiciary Committee began confirmation hearings, but no vote had been taken when the Senate recessed on December 16 at the and of the 96th Congress. On December 31, while the Senate was in recess, Carter made Heen a recess appointee. Carter's action came almost two months after he lost to Ronald Reagan. A month after the recess appointment, on January 21, 1981, President Reagan withdrew Heen's nomination and he continued to sit as a district judge until December 16, 1981, when the first session of the 97th Congress ended.

While Judge Heen sat as a recess appointee, Janet Woodley was indicted on a drug charge and filed motions to suppress evidence allegedly obtained in violation of the Fourth Amendment. On November 16, 1981, Judge Heen denied the suppression motions and presided over a trial at which Woodley was found guilty. Woodley challenged Heen's authority to decide these matters as a recess appointee.

---

[96] *United States v. Allocco*, 305 F. 2d 704, 706 (2d Cir. 1962), cert. denied, 371 U.S. 964 (1963).
[97] Id. at 708-09.
[98] Id. at 709.
[99] Id. at 712.
[100] John S. Castellano, "A New Look at Recess Appointments to the Federal Judiciary – *United States v. Allocco,*" 12 Cath. U.L. Rev. 29 (1963).

In 1983, a three–judge panel of the Ninth Circuit decided this case by analyzing the inherent tension between the President's Article II recess appointment powers and the attributes of judicial independence incorporated into Article III. It held that "only those judges enjoying article III protections may exercise the judicial power of the United States."[101] Only an "even more explicit constitutional provision" could override the values in Article III, and the general language of the recess appointment clause, which "does not mention the judicial branch at all," was insufficient to overcome the command of Article III.[102] The court's review of the records and writings of the constitutional period highlighted the importance of judicial Independence to the framers.[103] It also noted that decisions by the Supreme Court have emphasized the importance of an independent judiciary.[104]

The Justice Department argued that the "long and accepted" practice of the President making recess appointments to Article III courts had created an "historical consensus." The court acknowledged that there had been 283 previous recess appointments to the federal bench — six of them to the Supreme Court — and yet also stated that the practice "fell into disuse a generation ago." Judge Heen's appointment in 1980 "was the only recess appointment in the past twenty years."[105] Although both the legislative and executive branches had long accepted the President's power to make recess appointments to the federal bench, and officials in the two branches swear to uphold the Constitution, "the courts alone are the final arbiters of its meaning."[106]

The Ninth Circuit reviewed a number of decisions that had given great weight to historical practice and the constitutional interpretations reached by the political branches. However, it said that line of reasoning no longer "represents the thinking of the Court," especially after *INS* v. *Chadha* (1983) struck down a 50-year experiment with the legislative veto.[107] Following the reasoning in *Chadha,* which ruled that convenience and efficiency were subordinate values to constitutional commands, the court concluded that to whatever degree recess appointments to judgeships contribute to judicial efficiency, they "offend the explicit and unambiguous command of article III that the judicial power be

---

[101] *United States v. Woodley*, 726 F. 2d. 1328, 1330 (9th Cir. 1983).
[102] Id. at 1331.
[103] Id. at 1331-32
[104] Id. at 1334-35.
[105] Id. at 1336.
[106] Id.
[107] Id. at 1337.

exercised only by those enjoying life tenure and protection against diminution of compensation."[108]

A majority of the Ninth Circuit voted to rehear the case en banc.[109] In 1985, the full court held that the President may constitutionally confer temporary federal judicial commissions during a recess of the Senate. Judge Heen could therefore constitutionally preside over a criminal trial. The court, divided 7 to 4, decided that there is "no reason to favor one Article over the other."[110] Article II explicitly gave the President the power the fill "all" vacancies during a Senate recess, and there was "no basis upon which to carve out an exception from the recess power for federal judges."[111] The court noted that Presidents had made approximately 300 judicial recess appointments and that Congress "has consistently confirmed judicial recess appointees without dissent."[112] The court further noted that Rutledge was not confirmed, but the Senate rejected him not because he was a recess appointee but because of his speeches against the Jay Treaty.[113]

As to the importance of *Chadha,* the court noted that the legislative veto is "a recent practice, barely 50 years old," whereas recess appointments to federal courts "reach back to the days of the Framers."[114] Considerable weight is given to unbroken practices "acquiesced in by the Framers of the Constitution when they were participating in public affairs."[115] Since a recess appointee lacks life tenure and in not protected by salary diminution, the individual "is in theory subject to greater political pressure than a judge whose nomination has been confirmed."[116] However, "[e]ven viewing the recess clause as an unwise constitutional provision, it is not for this court to redraft the Constitution. Changes in that great document must come through constitutional amendment, not through judicial reform based on policy arguments."[117]

Judge Heen served out his recess appointment, which lasted until the end of the first session of the 97th Congress. President Reagan did not nominate him to a lifetime appointment. Heen left the federal court to sit on the Hawaii State Intermediary Court of Appeals.[118] Because of Carter's defeat by Reagan, Heen

---

108 Id. at 1338.
109 *United States v. Woodley*, 732 F. 2d 111 (9th Cir. 1984).
110 *United States v. Woodley*, 751 F.2d 1008 (9th Cir. 1985), cert, denied, 475 U.S. 1048 (1986).
111 Id.
112 Id. at 1011.
113 Id. at 1010, n.5.
114 Id. at 1011.
115 Id. at 1012.
116 Id. at 1014.
117 Id.
118 "U.S. Judge's Recess Appointment Ruled Illegal," *National Law Journal*, December 26, 1983, at 15.

said he knew his service on the federal bench would be short–term. He concluded that the recess appointment in his case was "an exercise in futility [because] you know you're not going to be around."[119]

Four law review article analyzed the *Woodley* case. Two of the articles, responding to the panel decision, argued that recess appointments to federal courts are a valid exception to the Article III requirements for life tenure and no-diminution.[120] The other two, written after the en banc ruling, concluded that recess appointments to the federal judiciary contravene Article III requirements and argued that recess appointees may not exercise Article III powers.[121]

However one analyzes the decision of the Ninth Circuit, sitting en banc, it stands only for the proposition that if the President and the Senate agree to recess appointments for federal courts, the appointments are not constitutionally invalid. The decision does not mean that the President and the Senate are forced in any way to accept recess appointments to federal courts as the preferred or even acceptable course. The two political branches could decide, on either political or constitutional grounds, that the recess appointment power should not be applied to the judiciary.

GREGORY'S APPOINTMENT

On the last day of the 106th Congress, December 15, 2000, with the Senate about to adjourn sine die, Senate Majority Leader Trent Lott voiced concern about the President's use of recess appointments, "especially appointments to the Federal Judiciary."[122] Senator Byrd cautioned that the Recess Clause "is not put in there to enable any President, Republican or Democrat, to play games with the Senate, or to attempt to do a one-upmanship simply because the Senate is out of session." He said he "especially hope[d]" that the Administration would not attempt "to fill a Federal judgeship during the recess of the Senate," and that he would not support "any administration, Democratic or Republican, that attempts to fill Federal judgeships while the Senate is in recess." Lott added that he had not

[119] "Recess Appointee Says It's Not a Great Idea," *Washington Post*, November 8, 1999, at A19.

[120] Thomas A. Curtis, "Recess Appointments to Article III Courts: The Use of Historical Practice in Constitutional Interpretation," 84 Colum. L. Rev. 1758 (1984); Joann Gaona, "Recess Appointment Power – Exception to or Violation of Article III," 1984 Ariz. St. L.J. 783 (1984).

[121] Paul Ferris Solomon, "Answering the Unasked Question: Can Recess Appointees Constitutionally Exercise the Judicial Power of the United States?," 54 Cinc. L. Rev. 631 (1985); Virginia L. Richards, "Temporary Appointments to the Federal Judiciary: Article II Judges?," 60 N.Y.U.L. Rev. 702 (1985).

[122] 146 Cong. Rec. S11833 (daily ed. December 15, 2000).

been notified of nay recess appointments "or any Federal judicial appointment during this recess period." He agreed with Byrd that "any appointment of Federal judge during a recess should be opposed." In recalling the Eisenhower recess appointments to the federal courts, Lott said that "was a mistake then, and it would be one now."[123]

President Clinton had nominated Roger L. Gregory to the Fourth Circuit on June 30, 2000.[124] On December 27, he announced Gregory's recess appointment, the first time since 1980 that President had named an Article III judge as a recess appointee. Clinton offered several reasons for his decision. He said that the U.S. Judicial Conference had declared the seat "a judicial emergency" and that it had been vacant for more than a decade. He regarded it as "unconscionable that the fourth circuit, with the largest African-American population of any circuit in our Nation, has never had an African-American appellate judge." Having offered nominations in the past for this vacancy, without obtaining confirmation from the Senate, he decided that a recess appointment was justified.[125] Clinton said he had "tried for 5 years to put an African-American on the fourth circuit."[126]

Press reports put the Gregory recess appointment in a larger context. Newspaper accounts described efforts by the Clinton White House to "put the Senate's record on black judges in play in the midst of controversy over President – elect Bush's attorney general nominee, Sen. John D. Ashcroft, who has been roundly condemned by civil rights groups for torpedoing the nomination of another African-American judicial candidate, Missouri Supreme Court Justice Ronnie White."[127] Other reports suggest that the decision to put Gregory on the court as a recess appointee was made before Election Day.[128] Rep. James E. Clyburn, chairman of the Congressional Black Caucus, stated that if Senate Republicans tried to remove Gregory, racial representation on the federal bench "would be an even bigger issue in the mid-term elections than it already is."[129] Another news story interpreted the recess appointment as not only placing the first black on the Fourth Circuit but "one also carefully calculated to create political difficulties for the Republican Party."[130]

Senator Inhofe, announcing that he would block any effort to confirm Gregory for a lifetime appointment, called it "outrageously inappropriate for any

[123] Id. at S11834.
[124] 36 Weekly Comp. Pres. Doc. 1564 (2000).
[125] Id. at 3180.
[126] Id. at 3182.
[127] "Clinton Names Black Judge to Appeals Court," *Washington Post*, December 28, 2000, at A8.
[128] "4th Circuit Surprise" Legal Times, January 1, 2001, at 6.
[129] "Clinton Names Black Judge to Appeals Court," *Washington Post*, December 28, 2000, at A8.
[130] "Clinton Names A Black Judge: Skirts Congress," *New York Times*, December 28, 2000, at A1.

president to fill a federal judgeship through a recess appointment in a deliberate way to bypass the Senate."[131] It was reported that Senator Lott had told Clinton he would oppose any recess appointments of judges.[132]

On January 3, 2001, President Clinton renominated Gregory for the 107th Congress.[133] On March 19, President George W. Bush withdrew the names of 10 nominees for federal judgeships, including Gregory.[134] In the meantime, the Senate and the White House negotiated over the procedures for acting on judicial nominees. By early May, it was reported that Senate Democrats said they would not agree to confirmation votes for Theodore B. Olson as Solicitor General and Larry Thompson as Deputy Attorney General unless the Republicans restored the right of individual Senators to block judicial nominations from their home states. They also said they would block action on any judicial nomination until the issue was resolved.[135] In what was interpreted as a conciliatory move, President Bush announced eleven nominations for the federal judiciary on May 9, including the name of Roger Gregory for a lifetime appointment to the Fourth Circuit.[136]

The Senate Judiciary Committee cleared Gregory on July 19 by a vote of 19 to 0.[137] On the following day, the Senate approved Gregory 93 to 1, the sole negative vote coming from Senator Lott.[138] Although there was no floor statement by Senator Lott, the media quoted his spokesman saying that his opposition to Gregory was "an institutional decision" designed to protect Senate prerogatives and emphasize his position that "any appointment of federal judges during a recess should be opposed."[139] During the floor debate, Senator George Allen spoke in favor of Gregory but did not want his support interpreted as condoning "the former President's political manipulations" and the "past procedural aggravation."[140]

[131] "Senator Vows He Will Fight Clinton's Judicial Selection," *New York Times*, December 29, 2000, at A15.

[132] Id.

[133] 37 Weekly Comp. Pres. Doc. 4-5 (2001).

[134] 37 Weekly Comp. Pres. Doc. 503 (2001); "ABA's Role in Vetting U.S. Judges Is Reviewed," *Washington Post*, March 20, 2001, at A1.

[135] "Democrats Block Picks for 2 Justice Posts," *Washington Post*, May 4, 2001, at A10.

[136] 37 Weekly Comp. Pres. Doc. 724-25 (2001); "Bush Will Nominate 11 as U.S. Judges," *Washington Post*, Mary 9, 2001, at A1.

[137] Panel Clears Judge Gregory, Two Others," *Washington Post*, July 20, 2001, at A2.

[138] 147 Cong. Rec. S7992 (daily ed. July 20, 2001).

[139] "Senators Confirm 3 Judges, Including Once – Stalled Black," *New York Times*, July 21, 2001, at A28.

[140] 147 Cong. Rec. S7991 (daily ed. July 20, 2001).

Conclusions

Despite ligitation in *Allocco* and *Woodley,* the President's use of recess appointments for federal judges remains an unsettled constitutional issue. The President's appointment powers under Article II are in tension with the Senate's confirmation role and with the constitutional guarantees to federal judges under Article III. The issues identified by senator Hart in his 1960 resolution are still with us. Individuals placed on Article III courts for an interim period lack the independence of judges who are given life tenure and are protected against diminution of salary. Recess appointees weaken the advice and consent role of the Senate and, some believe, diminish the constitutional protections accorded to litigants.

As a result of the controversy over the Eisenhower recess appointments of Warren, Brennan, and Stewart, there appears to be a political agreement that the President should not use recess appointment powers for Justices of the Supreme Court. After President Carter's appointment of Judge Heen, there seemed to be a similar agreement for lower court judges. Because of President Clinton's appointment of Judge Gregory, the dispute over recess appointments for district courts and the federal circuits has been rekindled.

The Senate can issue sense-of-the-Senate resolutions and other non-binding statements, but it cannot prevent the President from invoking the recess appointment power to appoint federal judges. However, the issue is as much subject to political checks and understandings as it is to judicial rulings. The Senate always has the option of making it clear that such interim appointments would be defeated overwhelmingly when the individual is nominated for a lifetime appointment. Should it do so, it would give notice that such appointees could expect limited tenure. Presidents would then decide whether it is worth the laborious process of completing background checks on nominee and interviewing them, merely to put judges on the court for brief periods.

SELECTED REFERENCES

Carrier, Michael A. "When Is the Senate in Recess for Purposes of the Recess Appointments Clause?," *92 Michigan Law Review 2204* (1994).

Castellano, John S. "A New Look at Recess Appointments to the Federal Judiciary – *United States v. Allocco,"* 12 Catholic University Law Review 29 (1963).

Chanen, Stuart J. "Constitutional Restrictions on the President's Power to Make Recess Appointments," *79 Northwestern University Law Review 191* (1984).

Curtiss, Thomas A. "Recess Appointments to Article III courts: The Use of Historical Practice in Constitutional Interpretation," *84 Columbia Law Review 1758* (1984).

Gaona, Joann. "Federal Courts — Recess Appointment Power — Exception to or Violation of Article II," *1984 Arizona State Law Journal 783* (1984).

Note. "Recess Appointments to the Supreme Court — Constitutional But Unwise?," *10 Stanford Law Review 124* (1957).

Richards, Virginia L. "Temporary Appointments of the Federal Judiciary: Article II Judges?," *60 New York University Law Review 702* (1985).

Solomon, Paul Ferris. "Answering the Unasked Question: Can Recess Appointees Constitutionally Exercise the Judicial Power of the United States?," *54 Cincinnati Law Review 631* (1985).

U.S. Congress. House Committee on the Judiciary, "Recess Appointments of Federal Judges," 86th Cong., 1st sess. (Committee Print, January 1959).

——. Senate Committee on the Judiciary, "Expressing the Sense of the Senate that Recess Appointments to the Supreme Court of the United States Should Not Be Made Except Under Unusual Circumstances," *S. Rept. No. 1893, 86th Cong., 2nd sess.* (1960).

——. Subcommittee on General oversight and Investigations of the House Committee on Banking and Financial Services, "The Termination of Mr. Robert H. Swan as a Member of the Board of the National Credit Union Administration, *104th Cong., sess.* (1966).

INDEX

A

B

C

Q

R

S

T

U

V

W